THE STRONGEST YOU

IVANA STRASKA SZAKAL

 England

The Strongest You

All rights reserved. No parts of this book may be reproduced, scanned or distributed in any printed or electronic form without the written permission of the author. Please do not participate in or encourage piracy of copyrighted material in violation of author's rights. Purchase only authorized edition.

Neither the author nor the publisher is engaged in rendering professional advice or service to the individual reader. Information in this book is intended to educate and is not to substitute consulting with medical professionals. All matters regarding your health require medical supervision. Neither the author nor the publisher shall be liable or responsible for any loss or damage allegedly arising from any information or suggestion in this book.

First edition

ISBN 978-1-9998266-0-4

Graphic design by Christopher Gill

Copyright © 2017 by Ivana Straska Szakal

Published by IVANA, England

THE STRONGEST YOU

When the little things in life seem difficult to cope with; when everything and everyone seem to be against you; when life just seems hard, read this book and remember this simple phrase:

"In the mind and self, be The Strongest You".

Use the strength within you to enjoy life and simply being you. Learn to promote positive thoughts, improve feelings and achieve your full potential.

THE STRONGEST YOU

THE STRONGEST YOU

This self-help book shares an unconventional approach that helps create unique results in life and which any person can adopt to achieve beneficial change. The book introduces coaching of the mind towards positive transformation. The reader resets the mind in less than 12 weeks to step on the path towards joyfulness.

The book incorporates mental imagery audio tracks to activate the desired adaptation of the brain. The reader is carried forward while intentionally using techniques tailored to their circumstances. Powerful techniques are learned, such as visualization, restructuring of thinking, emotional reprocessing, mindfulness, relaxation and more.

THE STRONGEST YOU

MANY THANKS

Life has always brought me people who, in one way or other, nudge me towards becoming a wiser and better person. Sometimes paths cross briefly, other times people stay longer, giving and taking. We share our lives and then walk our separate routes.

I want to express my appreciation for their sharing and leaving their imprints on me, enriching my life. I do my very best to use all that I gained from them to help others.

I am deeply thankful for family and friends who have stayed with me through difficult times, those who have supported me and helped me not to give up and return the joy of life.

How can I express my gratitude for encouraging me to write this book, to share my knowledge and experience? I cannot thank enough Chris, Silvia and Samo!

THE STRONGEST YOU

PREFACE

My personal history in many ways distressful and painful helped me to become who I am. When my life lost momentum, when caught unprepared and exposed to traumatizing stress and loneliness, I was hitting rock bottom. The approach I share through this book became a life saver. It helped me to come to terms with difficult challenges, carry on with life and continue to help others. Challenges have eventually turned into powerful, meaningful confrontations, thanks to the approach which is the subject of this book.

My journey towards this book started at the beginning of my career. Many times facing the demands of life we find it difficult to be content, and craving for good feelings never stops. Desire to be happier is within us and we might struggle to know how to pursue it. With the application of appropriate techniques we can spring back.

I decided to write a self-help book with guided practice, perhaps not quite a usual format. I am concerned about the lack of accessible, easy to follow self-help books, acting as guidance on how to approach ourselves, even if we don't suffer difficult to manage conditions. We all experience stress at some point, abrupt challenges and losses brought by life. With the right tools we can get through difficulties more easily.

Perhaps thanks to my own circumstances I redirect attention from what we can't do to what we can do. Put attention to the right place. Simply know ourselves and from there move towards improvement.

I have always believed in a psycho-educational approach, when an individual becomes actively involved. Keeping their motivation high I assign small experiments for the clients to do alongside working with me. This helps to stay on track towards change, increasing their control and choosing direction. With this in mind I combine knowledge with techniques in writing this book.

There is not much use of knowledge without its application. Practise is also to reverse the automatic mode of the mind while utilizing existing limits, resetting the mind and letting it functionally serve. Practical aspects allow the development of essential skills while experiencing the impacts of displayed actions.

Based on my understanding of the mind I have included guided mental imagery and application of mindfulness to emphasize the effects of an involved approach.

The book is divided into two parts:

Part One, stemming from cognitive (thinking) and behavioural theories, explains the impact of the mind on feelings, actions, decisions and choices. It discusses how the mind influences the relationships to oneself, others and the world.

There are distinctive parts prompting the reader to curiously elaborate and experiment. As the reader is carried forward they learn how their personal history has affected their experience. They learn how their beliefs change their perception and interpretation of every day occurrences. The informative aspects of Part One lead to the practical application within each chapter.

Part Two goes deeply into specific techniques, reasoning behind them and advising how to apply them. These techniques should allow emotional reprocessing and restructuring the mind. They are easy to apply, motivational and positively affecting the reader.

I consider a variety of issues that might be resistant to analytical and logical thinking. Here I bring guided mental imagery allowing relief of unwanted feelings and beliefs. Sabotaging behaviour frequently stays in the way of advancement. For that reasons I involve behavioural experiments to display new behaviour associated with positive attitude.

Appendix of this book includes illustrations, tables, charts and pictures. The reader is advised to obtain downloadable and printable material from:

- Worksheets through - www.thestrongestyou.net/worksheets
- Audio tracks through - www.thestrongestyou.net/audio
- Author's resources through - www.thestrongestyou.net

MY STORY BEHIND THIS BOOK

When my world fell apart, when the life I thought was stable and secure collapsed like a house of cards, I had no one to turn to. I had always been the strong person, my ethos in life was to support and help those I loved, my children, my husband, my friends, and as a professional psychotherapist, to help my clients. My own wellbeing was not something I considered, it was secondary and perhaps taken for granted or even disregarded. I became stressed when I didn't meet my expected goals and, not wanting to appear selfish, I worried about what others might think of me. Like so many people in the world I juggled my daily responsibilities of family, work and professional development. I was accommodating the needs of others while neglecting my own personal needs and desires. When my crisis came I was devastated. Traumatized and unprepared I did not know where to turn. My occupation and education should have given me the insight to cope but in my depths of despair I needed something more. I had to find a way of taking control and find the strength to rebuild my life; to rediscover the feelings of joy and happiness.

The dynamics of my life began to change with my children moving out to begin their years at university. I suffered as all parents do at this time, we experience a form of grief and initially struggle to fill the void left by their sudden departure. We want our children to be independent; we encourage and try to prepare them for it, but it doesn't soften the loss when they go. Everyone will find different ways of coping and I worked longer hours. It meant spending more time alone for myself, and I began doing some of the things I didn't have time for before. My husband was spending more time away from me with work or friends. I did some voluntary work and I believed that perhaps these changed circumstances were a positive step forward on the rocky road of life. I still had no idea of the impending crisis.

After 26 years of married life, without warning, my husband decided to leave me. Marriage is never without ups and downs but ours I believed had been good. I was not aware of any unresolvable issue. My husband was my partner, my best and lifetime friend, he was my companion and the rock that kept my spirit high through difficult times.

The breakup of a marriage breaks not only the partnership but also the family bond, the bond that has meant security for all. I was torn apart, the future was a black hole, the present was a nightmare that I could not wake up from. I felt physically ill, my body ached, the trauma and stress was taking its toll. Emotionally drained and desperately miserable I tried to continue working, listening to clients problems, advising them, helping them, but the effort wasn't enough. I had to take time off work and this made my situation even worse. Life was rapidly going downhill with no certainty of what might lie at the bottom.

In my sadness and despair I pushed away friends, those who had once been close I could no longer communicate with. Others suffering similar experiences and believing they had all the answers offered advice, I couldn't respond. I was drained emotionally and physically. I couldn't take pleasure in anything and I didn't understand myself. Believing I must be in some way to blame for my circumstances I didn't like my life. I wasn't coping.

In solitude the values, emotions, beliefs and bonds that I had nurtured for most of my life were challenged. Being totally alone felt safe yet I could see through the fog of sadness and in my heart I longed for change. I wasn't prepared to live in constant despair, I wanted to climb out of the abyss and into the light. I wanted to be happy again.

I missed my work, I often thought about the clients I had helped, people that had suffered but through my guidance and help had moved forward. I remembered their appreciation and gratitude, and then I wondered if the techniques successfully applied to them could be developed into self-help that I could apply to myself. I began to see a positive turn coming to my life if I just motivated myself and practised. I had nothing to lose. I started practising. With determination I dedicated time, energy and focus to move towards my goal. I opened up to welcome positive change in my life. Connected with my mind and feelings I was on the journey towards improvement. My emotional attachments and judgements made it uneasy. I allowed honesty and confrontation with my own beliefs. My resistance to feel good was surprisingly strong but step-by-step I restructured my mind. Accepting the truth was quite difficult and truthfulness brought unpleasant memories. I needed to reprocess my old emotions and let go of my painful past.

It was difficult to advance without feeling sorry for myself or feeling angry at those who hurt me, and I didn't fight these feelings, I used them. It was not easy and there was unavoidable daily sweat and tears. I allowed compassion and kindness. I practised mindfulness, forgiveness and non-judgemental thinking. I let go of the resistance to feel good. My daily practise developed into a remarkable transformation. I reset my mind. I stopped fixating on the negative or on my interpretations of past circumstances.

I now nurture a positive attitude when things don't go the way I wish. I mostly react efficiently to events and not to allow the worst becoming worse. I grow each day regardless of the happenings around me. When dealing with negativity I know what I have to do. I use my "trained" mind to constructively change the feelings. My relationships, including the one with myself, have a new quality. I try to consciously interpret the actions of others to intensify what I value. I foster trust, courage, gentleness and compassion. With a focused mind I find self-fulfilment through mindfulness. With my "trained" mind I generate the experience I choose. If I fail, I try it again, and again.

Perhaps the most positive consequence of my troubled history is this book. My approach, shared through these chapters, has become my new ethos. I present these techniques that proved so successful, with the intention of helping others create a positive and happy outcome, despite their sometimes difficult or stressful realities.

THE STRONGEST YOU

TABLE OF CONTENTS

PART ONE
THE HEALTHIER MIND, THE STRONGER YOU

1.	**A Good Start Is Half the Work**	**4**
	1. 1. My Time	4
	1. 2. Work with this Book	5
	1. 3. The Decision is Yours	9
	1. 4. Let's Do It Now	10
	1. 5. Resistance	11
	1. 6. Trouble Shooting	11
2.	**The Forces Within Us**	**12**
	2. 1. Negative Default of the Mind	12
	2. 2. The Mind Is the Power	13
	2. 3. Change What You Don't Like	13
	2. 4. Intentionally Restructure the Mind	15
3.	**The Power of the Mind**	**18**
	3. 1. The Powerful Mind	18
	3. 2. Awareness Starts in the Mind	19
	3. 3. Know Your Mind	21
4.	**Emotional Health and Happiness**	**26**
	4. 1. Good Feelings Make You Resilient	26
	4. 2. Are You Emotionally Healthy?	27
	4. 3. Truthfulness towards Emotional Health	30
	4. 4. Learn To Be Strong	32
	4. 5. Why Should You Care About Others?	33
	4. 6. Deal with Fears and Doubts	34
5.	**Build Self-Knowledge**	**38**
	5. 1. Relationships and You	38
	5. 2. Self-Induced Battles	39
	5. 3. Beliefs Get in the Way	40
6.	**The Mind over Feelings**	**42**
	6. 1. The Mind's Chatter	42
	6. 2. The Ways of Thinking	44
	6. 3. The Mind Lost in Feelings	46
	6. 4. Can You Be Sabotaged by Your Mind?	48

7.	**Understand Your Mind**	**50**
	7. 1. Development of Patterns of Thinking	52
	7. 2. What Fires Together, Wires Together	54
8.	**Strength in Emotions**	**58**
	8. 1. What Do We Know?	59
	8. 2. Three Components of Emotions	60
9.	**Towards Happiness**	**64**
	9. 1. Self-Reflection to Improve Feelings	64
	9. 2. Avoidance of Negative Emotions	66
	9. 3. What Can We Do?	67
10.	**Self-Esteem and Self-Compassion**	**70**
	10. 1. Good Thoughts about You	73
	10. 2. Why Self-Compassion?	75
11.	**Learn to Live with the Past**	**78**
	11. 1. Are Memories Changeable?	79
	11. 2. Personal Story and Feeling Good	80
	11. 3. Leaving the Past with Compassion	81
	11. 4. Mental Anticipation of Good or Bad	82
12.	**Don't Trust to Your Beliefs**	**86**
	12. 1. Understanding Beliefs	86
	12. 2. Beliefs about Yourself	87
	12. 3. False Self-Beliefs	88
13.	**Develop the Powerful Self-Image**	**100**
	13. 1. Impact of Self-Image	100
	13. 2. Trust to Feel Good	102
	13. 3. Happiness from Within You	106
	13. 4. Positive Reactions to Negative Events	108
14.	**Create Meanings and Goals**	**110**
	14. 1. Different Types of Personal Goals	110
	14. 2. Be Smart	113

PART TWO

KEEP PRACTISING TO BE THE STRONGEST YOU

15.	**Mindfully Reduce Stress**	**120**
	15. 1. Through the Powerful Mind	121

	15. 2. Actions to de-Stress	123
	15. 3. Communicate Assertively	126
	15. 4. Stressful Relationships	127
	15. 5. Technique to de-Stress: Use Focus	129
	15. 6. Mindful Breathing to Relax	130
16.	**Reset the Mind**	**132**
	16. 1. Change Self-defeating Thinking	132
	16. 2. Costs and Benefits of False Beliefs	135
	16. 3. When You Can't Change Beliefs	142
17.	**Mental Imagery to Strengthen the Mind**	**146**
	17. 1. Let the Mind and Brain Work	146
	17. 2. Powerful Mental Imagery	147
	17. 3. Try Self-Guided Mental Imagery	148
	17. 4. Grow with Mental Imagery	150
	17. 5. Can You Project the Future?	152
	17. 6. How to Enter Limitless Possibilities	153
18.	**Become Stronger through Mindfulness**	**156**
	18. 1. Understand Mindfulness	156
	18. 2. Learn Relaxation Techniques	159
	18. 3. Self-Fulfilment through Meditation	164
19.	**Non-Judgemental Thinking Can Help**	**170**
	19. 1. Letting Go of Judgements	170
20.	**Into Automatic Thoughts**	**172**
21.	**Don't Fixate on Negative**	**174**
	21. 1. Gratitude Techniques	175
	21. 2. Forgiveness Techniques	176
22.	**Practising Emotional Focus**	**180**
	22. 1. Technique to Reprocess Emotions	181
	22. 2. Let's Start	184
23.	**Last Helpful Hints**	**186**
About the Author		**190**
Appendix		**192**
Bibliography		**206**

THE STRONGEST YOU

PART ONE
THE HEALTHIER MIND, THE STRONGER YOU

THE STRONGEST YOU

1. A GOOD START IS HALF THE WORK

"If we are trained there is nothing which will not become easy. First, by training to tolerate minor problems, later, we become able to tolerate great problems."

~The Healing Power of the Mind by Tolku Thondup Rinpoche

While working with my struggling clients from various cultural and emotional backgrounds, and going through my own troublesome life, I have been confronted with the truth. We have poor self-knowledge, low self-awareness, too much negativity and few good feelings.

Behind faces we hide difficulties and struggles yet we say "I am okay" when asked how we are doing. We don't want others to know about our negative thoughts and difficult life turns. We hide that life becomes tough, that we are not getting through without falls or tears.

Often preoccupied by events in the outside world we live stressful lives, detached from nature and other beings. When we fail we might breakdown or hopelessly wait. We don't know how to respond to unfortunate circumstances or how to be alright when left alone.

We don't realize that disregarding minor problems could grow into an emotional roller coaster, not seeing opportunities that would make experiences happier or easier, neglecting what might be good for us. We do it because we don't understand ourselves. We don't know our own minds and how they manage our lives.

We might try to understand this complex world, technologies, sciences, politics, cultures, history and ignore the most powerful aspects: the mind and emotions shaping our life and staying with us at all times. Perhaps, we don't like this but really think about this: Why should someone else understand us when we don't understand ourselves? Why should someone else care for us when we don't do it ourselves? What if it is true that like attracts like? We become what we want to attract.

1. 1. My Time

The mind's negative default is the biggest reason why people don't feel good and resist being happy. Overcome it and the feelings can shift. We should feel worthy of living a happier life and do what has to be done to preserve good feelings.

We might think of happiness as something people pursue but the opposite is true. We must invite happiness into life by allowing ourselves to be happy, learning to be happy and cultivating good thoughts and feelings. This can't happen until we create conditions within ourselves, make happiness happen.

Time, Focus and Practice

Think about this: For twelve weeks twenty minutes daily can be so called "my time". Within these minutes you will allocate about ten minutes to reading and writing, and ten minutes to practising. Practise means you will turn audio tracks on, close your eyes and follow mental imagery as instructed. Then you will mark the Daily Activity Log and your daily session is completed. Next day you will do the same and continue where you finished the day before. How does it sound?

"My time" is the quality time given to improve the mind; to alternate its troublesome default and change feelings. In "my time" we learn and practise how to train the mind, modify beliefs and negativity, deliver kindness to our hearts, heal old hurts, cope with current relationships, understand personal strengths and limits.

"My time" is for creating valuable self-awareness. It deepens the connection with life experience. During this time we experiment to reprogramme the mind, build emotional resilience, create goals, identify needs, desires or wants, find meanings and project future direction. Learn compassion and gentleness towards the person we are, and boost good feelings about ourselves.

The ultimate goal of "my time" is: To advance through finding the internal strength to improve feelings thereby create a happier experience.

1. 2. Work with this Book

At sections called **Stop and Think** we pause and bring attention to discussed issues; become constructive, thoughtful, and here we:

- spend as much time thinking as we might need or wish.
- include personal experience and individual circumstances.
- use self-reflection, open-mindedness and honesty.
- try to connect with feelings.
- stay non-judgemental unless we are asked.
- are kind and patient with ourselves.

My Journal sections require genuine expression of thoughts and feelings. Journals are personal and confidential, they serve self-exploration. We must feel comfortable to freely and safely express genuine thoughts and feelings. Journal entries should steadily link up self-knowledge. There are a few reasons for handwriting:

- Handwriting allows better access to the psychological processes and thoughts.
- When we don't focus on spelling or language we increase validity of expression and no electronic devices can substitute this.
- The act of handwriting is a cognitive exercise that activates specific areas in the brain.
- Creative handwriting helps the development of new neurological connections in the brain.
- Self-reflection of emotions and thoughts written in journals becomes a valuable source to monitor what we do.
- Imaginative handwriting boosts creativity and can turn into a therapeutic experience of self-expression.
- Focus is on the content not the form; the form is irrelevant as long as we can read and understand what we write.

Immediate activities are marked as **Let's Do It Now**. These parts are inseparable from reading and we shouldn't continue until we finish these sections. Each part clearly states expectations, and even if we might prefer not doing, we should complete them.

Sections **Helpful Hints** provide additional help to comprehend. **Examples and Illustrations** deepen understanding of discussed topics. They might remind one's circumstances and thus, help how to apply knowledge to real life.

Practise is crucial to break habits, activate new behaviour, avoid procrastination, build consistency and persistence. For these reasons we work with printable sheets called the **Daily Activity Log** and monitor accomplishments. We check daily progress and compliance. We should also record what we don't do or skip. Although the logs are for the period of twelve weeks, we can use them in the future to advance while addressing personal challenges that go beyond the scope of this book.

Let's Do It Now

Print the Daily Activity Log for week #1 starting today. Continue printing one sheet per a week and mark them daily.

Daily Activities Log Week # __

	Day 1	Day 2	Day 3	Day 4	Day 5	Day 6	Day 7
Reading	✓ ✗	✓ ✗	✓ ✗	✓ ✗	✓ ✗	✓ ✗	✓ ✗
Journal	✓ ✗	✓ ✗	✓ ✗	✓ ✗	✓ ✗	✓ ✗	✓ ✗
Practice	✓ ✗	✓ ✗	✓ ✗	✓ ✗	✓ ✗	✓ ✗	✓ ✗
Total time							

Personal Statements:

Techniques / Tools:

Oops! Unplanned breach! What will I do to prevent it?

Weekly Summary

Positive Changes:

Unwanted Downfalls:

Oops! The negative mind! Strategy to overcome it in the future:

Throughout the period of twelve weeks the section "Practice" marks guided mental imagery as follows:

Week 1: Mindfulness in Breathing

Week 2-3: Allow Good Feelings

Week 4-5: Let Go of the Past

Week 6 -7: Acceptance

During the week # 8 to 12 we can incorporate any practice of personal choice such as mental imagery for relaxation, limitless possibilities, project future, techniques to access automatic thoughts. At this point we can practise other techniques such as emotional focus, gratitude, forgiveness, reprogramme the mind, etc.

1. 3. The Decision is Yours

Think about this: It is wise to put energy and time to the right place. People never know what the future holds but without the trained mind, emotional resilience, knowing self, identifying and satisfying needs, without meanings and being rooted in personal life, they can't turn chances into opportunities. Decide if you prefer the mind taking you wherever or train the mind to generate strengths and pursue what you desire.

Few Notes Before the Start

- Obtain a journal, index cards or sticky notes, and have access to an audio player and printer.

- Take it easy. Having a timescale of twelve weeks doesn't have to make you anxious. Stay relaxed about the deadline.

- The goal is to spend a maximum of twenty minutes daily, reading and practising. Let's call it daily sessions.

- The final goal is: Finish the twenty minute daily session during the next twelve weeks.

- Use daily activity logs and mark accomplishments.

- Commit to this book. Avoid reading and practising as the last thing in the day.

- Regularity is crucial and the mindset should be as if dealing with duties, taking care of health or helping a loving person.

- Mark daily sessions on a calendar. Schedule them two weeks in advance.

- Don't rush through reading or practise. Spend time reviewing what seems difficult before moving to the next parts.

- Within daily sessions maintain a positive attitude. Take micro-breaks when frustrated: stretch the body, open the window and take few controlled breaths, sip water or take a walk around the room.

- Always follow the schedule to achieve the daily total time.

- Create personal statements that help to generate a positive attitude.

- Stay kind and patient. Intentionally encourage confidence and trust to achieve daily goals.

- Don't allow giving up and whatever gets in your way deal with it directly.

- Maintain a private and quiet place to complete daily sessions.

1. 4. Let's Do It Now

Think about the reasons you are reading this. Why would you want to work with this book? You might think you want to feel better or understand yourself, learn techniques to improve personal life, know how to be more fulfilled, be grounded in life, or maybe someone gave you this book. Then bring attention to doubts and resistance. Answer: Why wouldn't you want to complete this book? Be honest, creative, open minded and try to recognize what might feed your resistance. Then get paper and pen. Divide the paper in two columns: Costs / Benefits. Write possible costs and benefits of completing your daily sessions throughout twelve weeks. Then compare and validate Costs / Benefits. Try to put them in a bigger perspective of time. Perhaps, put them in a scope of your life and their importance for the future.

1. 5. Resistance

People might object to the idea of improving oneself or say the lack of time doesn't allow them. Someone might say it's not the right time, they need better circumstances, they have to focus on other things such as job or children. Others might say it's impossible to change, believe in destiny, or think that people can't do much to have a better life. All of these thoughts come from the negativity of the mind. They feed the resistance to feel good.

Whatever resistance we might have, it comes from current values and beliefs that we find in ourselves. The truth is, we postpone, wait and miss opportunities because of the negative default of the mind.

1. 6. Trouble Shooting

This book is a self-help format and we should treat it as schoolbooks or manuals. It's a type of learning we try to take easy, enjoy, stay relaxed, curious and progress while practising.

When finding challenging sections we can review the main points and be sure we understand. At times of doubt, tiredness, being overwhelmed, or when the negative mind completely undermines the work, we should be aware of this, deal with it immediately.

It is important to remember that relaxed or neutral feelings are always better than pushing ourselves. We benefit more with a positive attitude towards what we learn. We should try to stay flexible and accept even if we don't like something. Try to put aside doubts, practise curiosity without fixating on difficulties. Sometimes we resist because we don't want to recognise the beneficial truth.

Let's Start...

2. THE FORCES WITHIN US

The mind's negative default is the biggest obstacle to people feeling good and so resisting being happy. Once we overcome it the feelings shift; we start feeling worthy of living a happier life and we do what we have to do to preserve good feelings.

Think about the statement: "From this day forward I will not pursue happiness, I will instead invite happiness into my life." Spend few minutes thinking about this statement and notice how it makes you feel.

My Journal

Write these two statements: "I am allowing myself to be happy. I am learning to be happy". Think about them and write your comments about them.

2. 1. Negative Default of the Mind

To understand why to start in the mind if we want to feel happier we need to think about our ancestors. They lived life in physical threats. This got hardwired into their brains and DNA. This negative bias they passed down the generations to us.

Our ancestors also had to constantly scan the environment to survive and pay attention to what threats they were dealing with to distinguish real from their imagination. Thus, along the negative default it was awareness that got hardwired in brains and passed down to descendants, to us.

As we will later learn this genetically encoded information, awareness and negativity hardwired in the brain, is wrongly used these days. We can try to fix it and make it working properly. To do this we use the adaptability of the brain, so called neuroplasticity of the brain, which means "use it or lose it".

The change will happen once we use the brain's adaptability for our benefit. We will stop using the automatic mode of the mind to hardwire the default out. By conscious practise we can change hardwired negativity and false awareness. It can be extremely motivating to remember that practising literally rewires the brain for increased happiness. And that's why we have to maintain discipline throughout the next weeks.

2. 2. The Mind Is the Power

The automatic mode of the mind without our consent can push away happy feelings and we want to know when and how this happens. We sense what makes us feel good but because we don't understand the mind and we disconnect from personal life, we don't do much with it.

Some people notice their lives go in circles and they have repeated experiences, though different in details. They might feel like doing the same over and over, similar mistakes and choices, or pottering their days away. Others might be too focused on their future and let the present just pass through. Some people can't wait until their children grow up, get a new job, get a new house, have successful business or make better money. We fixate too much on results and don't notice what makes a real difference, the process of creating them.

Because by default the mind tends to hold on to the negative we experience fears or doubts growing from "what if". We might imagine that something in the future will go wrong. In one way or other, we detach from present moments. We have to shift awareness by connecting with current moments, mindfulness and development of self-knowledge.

Mindful means to experience the now rather than fixate on the future or past. The more we make efforts to bring awareness to present experiences, the more we find ourselves spontaneously recognizing and accepting; eventually noticing what we overlook. The mind takes us towards better experience through self-knowledge and conscious decisions. Gently changing what occupies the mind and thus correcting its default.

2. 3. Change What You Don't Like

Andy Warhol said, "They always say time changes things, but you actually have to change them yourself". Truly, changes don't happen on demand. We wish that what we want could happen overnight but the mind doesn't work that way. Changes happen in stages and they require effort and time.

Let's Do It Now

Print the dowloadable graph illustrating the process of changes. Review its parts and think about them. If you have any thoughts write them in your journal. Keep the graph visible during next weeks.

The process of change is the growth from the unknown to living changes, experiencing them and carrying on with them.

If we want changes to happen we must be willing to put enough effort, energy and time allowing them to happen. We have to last long enough, not give up too early, not to be overly eager at the start subsequently lose motivation quickly, or when obstacles and barriers arrive. Resetting the mind is precisely like that: it needs awareness, commitment, energy, focus, patience and time.

Helpful Hints

Do you find yourself failing New Year resolutions or commitment to something and never seeing it through? It takes approximately twelve weeks of regular and intentional commitment to break old habits and develop noteworthy changes. Almost anyone can restructure the mind: change the ways of thinking, break dysfunctional mental habits and create a positive attitude.

Illustration

Imagine you want to become a pilot and think how it could happen. It would need a lot of learning and practising, first with assistance before you sit in the cockpit and fly. There are costs involved when learning something and benefits when achieved.

Helpful Hints

We might go through battles before any accomplishment and before the default running mind responds. We shouldn't be afraid of doing it, taking bumpy roads or detours, taking us to our destination. We want to stay focused, firm, motivated, disciplined, and mostly don't give up.

2. 4. Intentionally Restructure the Mind

Greek philosopher Socrates said, "The secret of change is to focus all of our energy not on fighting the old but on building the new". Indeed, energy used for beating ourselves, or anger that life doesn't give us what we want, is a waste.

Living an unhappy life is draining, living in negativity we don't control. Better spent energy is to work towards gradual change.

We are not born to feel happy or unhappy; we just learn to see personal life through degrees of fortune. Thinking and emotions can be seen as generated abilities developed throughout life and under unique circumstances. This develops an automatic pilot of the mind that holds the resistance towards good feelings. Positiveness is the pilot's response to intentional restructuring.

There is not much we do to start. We shift focus, direct attention from the outside world to what happens inside of us. We have to learn how we respond to what happens to us. We try to find comfort in whatever kind of personal life we have today. We listen to our thoughts about us and the world.

Working on self-improvement always involves facing up to the truth and this can be hard. Nobody is perfect and we all have something we would like to hide, weaknesses or embarrassments, moments of shame or blame. The negative mind lacks compassionate thoughts, can't tolerate, it can be too critical. Necessary work is to improve what relates to us and how we respond to it.

Knowledge shouldn't make us feel worse and that's why we have to be gentle about shortcomings, become good and caring friends to ourselves. The strongest antidotes to negativity are kindness, compassion and a non-judgemental stance. Only with them we can recognize the truth or less appealing aspects and then improve.

Once the mind allows the worthiness of having positive experience, we become eager to overcome setbacks. Doubts or feelings of personal unimportance brought by the negative mind can get in the way. This narrowly relates to our interpretation of whatever happens to us.

How we understand the happenings of personal life matters a great deal.

Acceptance, respect and forgiveness are favours of the mind and they are powerful forces of growth. With gentle force, patience and care we can address beliefs that undermine our efforts to improve feelings and performance.

On the journey towards changes we should take small steady steps, notice accomplishments, give credits to ourselves and count every little progress. Positive expectations, courage and trust develop in a process of doing this.

Helpful Hints

Before something becomes significantly better it can get temporary worse and that's a critical point. Most people give up or stop. We can use personal statements to overcome frustration. Personal statements can be our anchors and should express what we want. They might sound like "I can feel good" or "I allow myself to improve the way I want". Each day we can feel better when we simply spent a few minutes focusing on these words.

My Journal

Recollect your thoughts about this chapter and try to capture your response, perhaps your ideas about the resistance to feel good. Think about the negativity and doubts. Do you think you can be happier? Do you have doubts? Why would you want to understand the mind and change its negative default?

Let's Do It Now

Write on an index card a simple personal statement expressing that you allow yourself to feel good. Keep this card with you. Copy it on a sticky note, post it somewhere visible, memorise it, repeat it each time when you doubt or you notice resistance to feel good.

THE STRONGEST YOU

3. THE POWER OF THE MIND

Unlike instincts which are inherent, feelings and thinking develop through life in a process of learning, associations and conditioning. They are not carved in stone and they can be changed as almost everything we developed in life. We have to remember: **Mental habits and feelings are changeable.** We can change them through self-knowledge and self-management.

3. 1. The Powerful Mind

Imagine a person fearful of darkness. To cope with their fear they might keep lights turned on in the whole house, they don't enter dark rooms or they don't go out after dusk. They notice feelings in their body caused by fear such as increased heart rate, lump in the throat, changes in breathing, might be shaky and sweaty, or they might feel discomfort in the stomach. They can also notice their thoughts, perhaps thinking about murders, criminals, the worst happening to them in the darkness, or they might think about negative personal experience.

To understand what is going on here we have to differentiate thinking, feeling and behaviour. Their experience starts with thinking about the darkness and interpretation of darkness. This generates their feelings, reactions in their body and emotions. They somehow behave to change emotions and compensate for unpleasant feelings. To cope with discomfort they do something.

Their behaviour seems logical because the darkness is a problem. But it is not completely true and there is much more happening.

It is not the darkness, a situation they are facing, but thinking about it that causes fear and reactions in their body. The behaviour, although compensating for their emotional discomfort, is dysfunctional, and in fact it maintains their fear of darkness. They don't deal with the problem and fear will grow again in response to their thinking and behaviour.

People unintentionally keep themselves trapped because of their mind and brain. Each time when their actions release uncomfortable feelings they reinforce connection of a situation - thinking – feeling – behaviour.

In the example fear is maintained by their thinking about darkness and their response to these feelings. Their repetitive dysfunctional behaviour hardwires fear in the brain. Their brain "works against" them and strengthens this cycle. To overcome fear of darkness they have to deliberately rewire their brain and change their thinking as a first step.

To improve feelings we must start with the mind, change what's going on in there to activate different reactions and behaviour.

We have to think somewhat differently to trigger desired physical and emotional reactions, modify actions and repeat all these to embrace neurological pathways in the brain. Repetition creates new associations and connections, it makes them automatic and hardwired in the brain. This way we can change almost anything we have developed in learning, associations, and conditioning.

Helpful Hints

The mind is a first responder to whatever situation. We think, thinking generates feelings and then, we do something in return. When we repeat the same the brain strengthens wiring and over time we don't consider it learned or developed, it becomes an automatic default.

3. 2. Awareness Starts in the Mind

A stream of thoughts generates feelings, bodily changes and behaviour.

The mind responds to any situation: meeting someone, talking on the phone, shopping, reading, driving, visiting friends, etc. At times we intentionally create situations, while other times they simply occur as a natural consequence. Some of these situations we experience as pleasant while others may be disturbing. Some of them we can control, while some depend on other people or circumstances.

Usually we are not mindful. We don't notice what triggers our thoughts but nearly always we can recognize feelings and actions. Lack of awareness of what we think, of what's going on in the mind, is the core of just making unconscious responses.

Mindfulness is full attendance, awareness; being fully present in a moment, noticing what happens in the mind and feelings. It helps to understand what and why we do what we do.

We might believe that changing conditions in the world around us can improve feelings. Indeed, it can work but it won't if we don't change our thinking and what we do in response. We have to reduce our focus on the outside world. Mindfulness is a technique redirecting attention from the world to ourselves and create new experience.

Many things around us are beyond our control but we must remember this: any time we can control thinking. We are in charge of how and what we think, how we interpret current experience and what we do with it.

Illustration

Example # 1: You are a driver who stopped in a traffic jam, you touch the golden necklace you recently inherited from a deceased grandmother. Vividly remembering the afternoon when you saw her the last time you think about happy holidays at her place. Missing her cheer and laughter makes you sad. Your eyes are teary. Your chest feels heavier and your breath is shallow. Then, a car behind you honks. You realise that traffic has moved. You turn on the radio to distract your thoughts.

What happened? A chain of reactions occurred. The mind reacted, thoughts instantly generated feelings, and you did something in response.

Example # 2: A voice message from your local clinic says that they want you to make another appointment as your blood test has to be redone. Your mind starts busily reviewing the reasons why. Depending on circumstances it triggers reactions and changes in the body. If you are healthy and the blood test was a routine check-up, you would probably think about mistakes on their side and would feel relaxed. If the blood test was done because you're sick, you would experience psychosomatic reactions, symptoms of sickness would feel more severe. Your thoughts and generated feelings would define your behaviour. Your reaction would depend on your thinking and how you interpret the message.

3. 3. Know Your Mind

The mind is constantly busy, activated by the world around us and within us, triggering reactions, emotions and actions.

Understanding how the mind, feelings and behaviour entwine is critical.

We should know how personal interpretations determine what we do in response to them, how we react and what we feel.

Have you realised how many choices you make every day? Every task, big or small, some conscious decisions and others run by default or automatic pilot.

Awareness, monitoring and regulation of thinking lead towards beneficial responses, improving situations and contributing to more powerful experience. We can't have total control over the mind; however, we can try as much as we can to positively influence what relates to us.

In real life we can't regulate most situations. We just respond to them and we want to respond mindfully. It is like when being thrown into wild waters we want to get out with control. With awareness we know that we have to swim.

Stop and Think

Think about one decision or choice that you made today. Can you remember how thinking lead towards it? Why did you do what you did? How did your feelings affect what you did? Was your choice deliberate or you decided automatically? How did your interpretation of a situation influence the choice and action?

Helpful Hints

We don't have to understand psychology to train the mind and improve feelings. The awareness can grow into control. Learn how one's thinking, feeling and actions interact. Then determine what we can control.

Illustration

Look at the example how the mechanism possibly works:

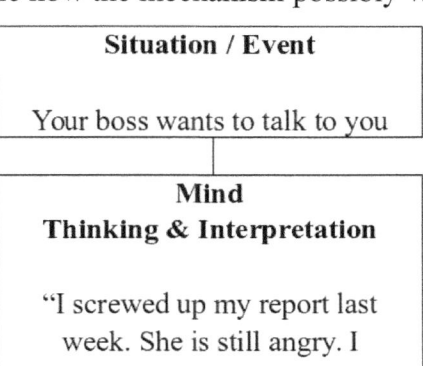

Situation / Event
Your boss wants to talk to you

Mind **Thinking & Interpretation**
"I screwed up my report last week. She is still angry. I apologized and now she is picking on me."

Bodily sensation / **Physical response**	**Emotions / Feelings**
Knot in stomach, pacing, tensing shoulders, clenching hands, gritting teeth, changes in breath, pounding heart, feeling flushed or sweaty, headache	Angry, scared, disappointed, hurt, confused, embarrassed, rejected, frustrated

Behaviour
Rapid walking to talk to a co-worker.

Let's Do It Now

Think about any situation that recently happened. Try to answer: Did you create it? Which parts of it did you deliberately influence? Which parts depended on you, on other people and circumstances? What was going in your mind? How were you feeling? What changes did you notice in your body? Did you feel different before, during and after this situation? Was it overall a pleasant experience? How did it affect your perception of the day as a whole?

In response to the situation fill in the chart:

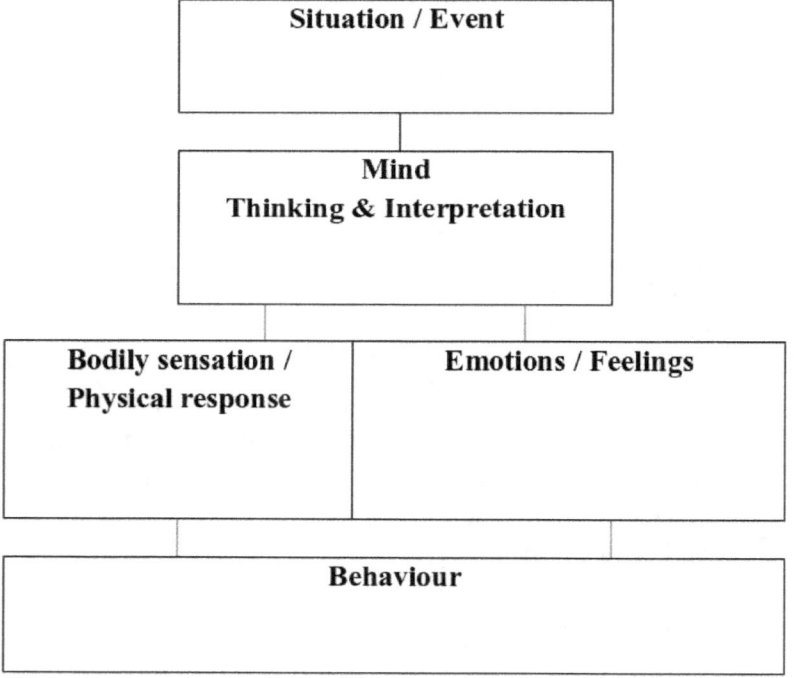

My Journal

Copy the previous chart to your journal and complete it. Analyse at least two different situations, one positive and one negative. Then copy the following chart and fill it in. This chart is to better understand what possibly happens when you respond to a situation. Try to be specific.

Situation – describe what happened, who was involved, where, why and when this happened:
Thinking – specify your self-talk just before and during the situation; your thoughts, mental images, expectations, judgements, beliefs:
Feelings and emotions – what you felt in the body; what emotions and how strong they were:
Your interpretation of the situation and behaviour of others – how you understood reactions of others and yours:
Identify aspects of your control and what depended on others:
What else could you have thought and done?

THE STRONGEST YOU

4. EMOTIONAL HEALTH AND HAPPINESS

Cultivating positive emotions and the strong mind can't be seen in isolation from the rest of us. They are incorporated in our overall health.

4. 1. Good Feelings Make You Resilient

Thanks to neurology and psychology we have a better understanding of the mind and brain. We know age is not as detrimental as we used to think, and improving the mind and feelings through intentional practise is possible and improving life.

Studies suggest that optimistic thinking and happy feelings are linked to good health. Bodies with happy minds fight stress or illnesses more easily. Fearful people, people suffering depression, trauma or anxiety are prone to suffer psychosomatically induced diseases such as migraine, back pain, autoimmune problems or gastro-intestinal problems, stomach or spleen difficulties.

The powerful mind and good feelings promote physical health and they are essentials of what is called emotional health.

Emotional health manifests in daily responses to life. We can think of it as a regulator of how well we cope with challenges, abrupt changes, how quickly and efficiently we respond to unpredictable situations or losses.

Emotional health is also about abilities to catch opportunities brought by life and turn them into positive successes.

We should be curious about characteristics of emotional health such as:

- self-esteem and self-compassion
- presence of optimism, positive self-perception, coping with everyday tasks with only a brief experience of downfalls
- perceived equality of physical and mental health, ability to preserve good feelings, lightness of being

- rooting in personal life, feelings of comfort, security and belonging
- quick adjustments, balanced hierarchy of needs and desires, flexibility of thinking
- efficient behaviour during ups and downs
- overall positive response to life for the best of one's psychological wellbeing.

4. 2. Are You Emotionally Healthy?

Emotional health is to buffer life challenges. We can't measure it but we can hint at its strengths. Positive emotions project stronger emotional health while distress, losses, disappointments, negligence or stress compromise it.

Emotional health is dynamic and by today's actions we should work on its improvement.

We can reflect on our current life and feelings to indicate whereabouts our emotional health is. When assessing emotional health we consider following areas:

- **Overall awareness** and building mental and emotional wellness, ability to capture imbalance and restore harmony, deliberate improvement of psychological weaknesses.
- **Positive responses** to difficulties without additional downfalls. Finding strength to stand up after falls. Courage to face difficulties or find meanings in crisis. Activation of prolonged optimism and capturing positive thoughts.
- **Overall resistance** to stress. Find lightness in unpredictable challenges or losses.
- **Acceptance, adaptability and adjustment** to unwelcome turns. Acceptance of feelings and emotions. Ability to boost positive emotions in distressful times.
- **Coping** well with rejections, failures or disappointments.

Respond to distress without additional damage of one's well-being.

- **Tolerance** of personal mistakes without significant emotional and mental disruption. Tolerate imperfection, mistakes and flaws.

- **Ownership and liability** for one's decisions, choices and actions. Take responsibility, learn from mistakes and move on. Self-correction to prevent future falls.

- **Flexible thinking and openness** to changes. Using mechanisms that build psychological flexibility. Constructive criticism and positive response to it.

- **Being truthful** with oneself and integration with personal values. Thoughts complementing feelings and actions.

My Journal

Copy the following chart and try to assess your emotional health. Use the information above.

Self-assessment of areas of emotional health:

Area	weak					strong				
	1	2	3	4	5	6	7	8	9	10
Awareness										
Positive responses										
Resistance										
Acceptance										
Adaptability										
Copying										
Tolerance										
Ownership										
Flexibility										
Truthfulness										

My Journal

Review characteristics of emotional health. Break them down into smaller and more specific characteristics of your emotional health. Develop a personal list of strengths and weaknesses.

Examples:

Strengths, characteristics of good emotional health:
I can quickly adjust after losses, Maintaining inner peace by regular meditation, Regular venting of emotions, Accepting limits and powers, Good self-expression of thoughts and feelings, I maintain positive attitude in distressful situations, I am a problem solver, I cope well with losses.

Weaknesses, characteristics of poor emotional health:
I am not aware of my feelings, I don't take care of my emotions, I often blow up, I have difficulties to stand up for my values, I am shy, Emotions block my thinking, I am a perfectionist, I take criticism too personally, I am devastated after making mistakes, Others manipulate me, I lack empathy, I have difficulties to maintain boundaries, I am anxious, I lack self-confidence, I can't let go and relax, I belittle myself, I fear rejection and conflicts.

4. 3. Truthfulness towards Emotional Health

Probably, everyone heard the buzz slogan "Let's be authentic". It encourages people to be unique and truthful.

Truthfulness with oneself refers to unity between thinking, feeling, saying and doing.

Inconsistency, acting differently around different people or trading one's integrity for being a likeable person for the costs of self-respect is very exhausting.

Truthfulness and showing the real side of oneself however, is not always easy. Honesty is risky, some people don't like it; perhaps wouldn't like us if we were fully truthful.

We must remember that loss of truthfulness makes us vulnerable, takes a high toll, and overtime we pay sky-rocketing tolls.

By the nature we want to be honest, being heard and suppressing the personal values is extremely frustrating. Frustration can grow in anxiety, anger, hostility, guilt or blame, and then for lost personal loyalty we pay a very high price. We disconnect from our needs and desires. We lose connection with others and can't create fruitful relationships. We perceive ourselves as victims not accountable for choices, and we find excuses for wrong behaviour. We can't cultivate good feelings.

We should be aware of the costs and benefits of lost integrity when loosing truthfulness with oneself and giving up personal values. To understand why we want to stand for what we believe, what we risk and what are the reasons when we abandon them.

My Journal

Choose a difficult person like those who you have trouble getting along with, they challenge you, put pressure on you or you suppress what you believe and don't allow yourself to be truthful around them. Think about how you react to them. Focus only on your reactions, not on them or their qualities. Honestly identify your feelings, thoughts and maybe distress you notice. Answer: How do you vent suppressed emotions and self-expression? What do you sacrifice to maintain this relationship? Why do you maintain this relationship? What is your position, expectations and boundaries in this relationship? How does your adjustment to this person affect overall your performance, emotions and relationships with others? What can you do differently?

Let's Do It Now

Remember a significant loss you experienced. For example abrupt loss of an important relationship, loss of job or money, health problems, being disciplined or facing the consequences of your wrong actions. Try to think about the details of it: when it happened, maybe why it happened, who was involved, what consequences it had on you and your life.

My Journal

Write about how well and fast you recovered from that loss. How quickly you were able to put yourself together and rebalance and feel good. Focus on emotions you experienced, the domino effect of that loss, how it affected other aspects of your life like relationships, social life, interests, sleep pattern, self-esteem, ability to relax, focus, performance, development of bad habits, avoidance or obsessions.

4. 4. Learn To Be Strong

Experiencing stressful times seems a painful reality of life. Distress can make our minds uncontrollable, prompting us to wrong decisions or self-sabotaging choices.

It is easy to get consumed when everything goes alright. We easily forget that we have limits and put too much on our plate. We probably sense it is wrong but mostly we keep going on or pushing ourselves beyond limits.

Distressful experiences make us weaker and vulnerable; when a sequence of bad happenings takes us down we should be alarmed. The awareness, efficiently copying with losses and learning from difficulties make us stronger.

The velocity of life leaves no break, without chance to relax we become fragile and the mind, once probably strong, wears down. We become less resistant, relationships get worse and we experience complex feelings that we can hardly understand. These come from the wrong mindset and attitude towards oneself. We have to change and prioritize psychological wellbeing. Try not to compromise our emotional and mental strength.

Don't wait until pushed beyond limits or burnt-out. Don't dwell in pity or sorry. Value emotional health as a part of overall wellness and proactively strengthen it.

 It is not easy to be resilient in difficulties or to stand up after falls, and that's why we create an extra supply of strengths beforehand by regular practise. Both, the body and mind need strength and flexibility to get through whatever in life.

Improvements don't happen by themselves and on demand. They happen in a process, effort and energy given to regular mental strengthening develops reservoirs of power before problems take their toll. Strong positive attitude buffers bumps at times of increased stress, losses, rejections, failures or disappointments.

Helpful Hints

We should realize that we are making choices. We either ignore personal welfare until circumstances crash us down or we commit to develop strengths, resilience and resistance. Doing so doesn't take much: treat oneself with respect, kindness, compassion and care, cultivate positive feelings, take responsibility for emotional wellbeing. Even during stress find time let go and relax and regularly recharge before life takes a downfall.

We don't buy new cars to improve the ones we already have. Routinely we maintain them, take them to mechanics for regular services to optimize their performance. Taking care of emotional health is not dissimilar. By not doing it, the negative default of the mind, the mind cluttered by dysfunctional thoughts, grows unwanted feelings. We become reactive and self-destructive.

My Journal

Stop and mindfully reflect: What stress level do you currently experience? What quality of relationships do you maintain? What do you need to do to promote emotional flexibility?

4. 5. Why Should You Care About Others?

Balanced relationships improve overall emotional wellbeing as they offer comfort and intensify security. We all long for good relationships but in reality most relationships are battles, and only few are fruitful. Good or bad relationships dramatically influence how we experience life, and they positively or negatively enrich one's life.

Knowing ourselves helps to identify what sort of attachments we

create and how we develop relationships.

We bring personal challenges into relationships and we should know them. If we struggle with emotions we might be easily manipulated, become objects of those who understand themselves better, become targets of bullies or narcissistic individuals. Self-knowledge allows identifying personal positions in relationships.

We can recognize toxic relationships, consciously deal with them and not let them compromise personal wellbeing. Carefully choosing the company of positive and supportive people, emotionally detaching from those who might undermine our welfare are important aspects of building healthy relationships.

It doesn't mean we give up others but with awareness we monitor and regulate attachments. "Like attracts like" can apply here. The best choice is to connect with like-minded people. The powerful mind and good feelings can be the right indicators of choosing people.

We can't change others but how we connect with them, how we let them affect us we can change anytime. Use awareness to identify who brings negativity, sadness or anger and put them in the right place in the mind. Based on personal welfare distinguish, prioritize and when circumstances work against us adapt, change the attitude or take additional steps to modify a relationship.

Helpful Hints

There are always people we clash with, don't like them, they don't like us, or we can't get along, yet we have to cope with them. They might be our family, coworkers or managers. Especially in these relationships we have to carefully monitor our emotional involvements. What we offer, what attention and thoughts, what feelings we give out and set appropriate boundaries. We should be responsible and accountable.

4. 6. Deal with Fears and Doubts

Negative feelings resulting from the negative default of the mind should be brought into attention because they always grow worse. The harmful mental habits are dwelling and ruminating. They almost always create fears and doubts. At this time the negative default of the mind takes over. We don't think flexibly and we can't see in a wide view. We neglect positive sides and fixate on the negative. This happens when we lose the reins and let the mind go wild. The only efficient response is to regain control and immediately manage thinking.

Fears and doubts can be seen as enemies created in the mind. Nothing feeds them more than dysfunctional and negative thoughts. Once we notice fears or doubts we have to deal with them. We don't want them to grow into monsters, creeping and undermining personal wellbeing. Instead of fears and doubts we need courage and trust.

Helpful Hints

Courage and trust are sources of positive attitude, strength, resistance and flexibility. They are integral components of emotional health. We can play games with ourselves. Imagine a coin and see fears and doubts as one side of it and trust and courage the other side. Anytime we can flip the coin and replace fear by courage, doubts by trust.

Let's Do It Now

There are no weaknesses that can't be improved and there are no strengths that last forever. We can use personal statements to urge the mind to cooperate. Think about the following personal statements and try to finish them:

- I am deliberately choosing good thoughts because _

- I regularly make time to laugh, relax and do something that gives me pleasure by doing ___

- When I feel fear I immediately stop and ask questions to understand what causes it. _

- I get emotional support from nourishing relationships with _

- I stop when I feel overwhelmed and spend time to regain calmness by doing _

- I put effort to maintain optimistic attitude by doing _

- Every day I take small steps to increase my self-acceptance by doing _

- I build awareness of my emotions and their triggers by doing _

- I recognize my feelings and feelings of others. I know this because _

- I accept my current limits which are _ and I work on overcoming them by doing _

- I honestly acknowledge my psychological weaknesses that are ____ and work on their improvement by doing __

- Awareness of my feelings helps me to_

My Journal

Considering the weaknesses of your emotional health and discussions in this chapter, create three personal statements to improve them. The personal statements should briefly and clearly express your intention. They should be believable and you shouldn't feel in conflict with them. Be creative, write statements then brainstorm their adequacy, correct them maybe a few times before finalizing them. Write three final statements on index cards and place them where you can frequently see them. Use mobile devices or computer and have them accessible. Read them frequently and do what they state until you personalize them.

Examples of statements: I assertively say no. When I feel fear I use curiosity to identify the reasons. I do small things every day that make my heart joyful. I meditate for five minutes every evening. I mindfully recognize and address my painful feelings. I vent my suppressed self-expression in my journal.

5. BUILD SELF-KNOWLEDGE

As we gradually develop self-knowledge we start connecting personal challenges with relationships we create. The negative default of the mind, difficulties related to insecurity, fears and stress make us vulnerable.

5. 1. Relationships and You

For many reasons positive emotions and mental resilience improve relationships. Emotionally balanced people become confident, generous, respectful, straightforward, predictable, secure, grounded. Because they feel good about themselves they are generous. They want others to feel good and that's what they bring into relationships.

Some people don't like accountability for relationships but liking it or not, we are accountable for relationships. We should acknowledge our portion when relationships are fulfilling or go downhill. It is not only the other party who makes a relationship good or bad. Each side brings something and decides what to offer or take. What we give out and disclose is a personal choice. We choose how far we go in a relationship when it goes wrong. We decide how much time we spend by thinking about it or by how much we allow a harmful relationship to compromise personal wellbeing.

If we want to change relationships firstly we must understand what emotional binding attaches us to the other parties. Secondly, we mindfully regulate these relationships.

Relationships can be stigmatized and charged with emotional prejudice, sometime rising from dysfunctional beliefs like "People should like me", "I shouldn't have conflicts with others", "Other first, then me", "Sacrifice yourself for others", "Be nice to everyone", etc. Surely, they can be nice principles but as core beliefs they can destroy personal welfare. They can't work in all circumstances and with all people, and with some people they never work. When analysing relationships we consider this.

Relationships should be intentionally adapted to personal wellbeing.

We should screen out what potentially contaminates wellbeing. Choose the company of people differently, and emotionally detach from those who might undermine our welfare. By noticing the kind of people we choose as friends we can recognise our beliefs and values.

5. 2. Self-Induced Battles

We don't want to be black and white and see unpleasant feelings as always wrongful. They are unavoidable, protective and also very human. There are many situations where we naturally have to feel them. A person who would not feel sad after losses would be at the very least strange, not feeling disappointed or angry when witnessing injustice would be abnormal.

We can't and shouldn't always try to avoid negative feelings. We can allow feeling negative emotions. However, these feelings can become uncontrollable when we fail to vent and regulate them.

We must allow experiencing negative emotions from time to time as a response to life. Also we have to distinguish negative feelings that result from the wrong mindset.

When noticing that we dwell or ruminate we have to interrupt the mind. Instantly and intentionally we break these mental habits. This way we train the mind to fixate on constituent elements. And we must do it again and again until the brain responds. Overtime the mind less frequently engages dysfunctional habits. It becomes easier and more automatic for the mind to notice that which is crucial and screens out insignificant aspects. Ultimately the mind and brain reset and develop new neurological pathways.

Illustration

We need to recognize when troublesome emotions result from harmful mental habits. The negative default of the mind stresses hardships and directs attention to wrong places. The efficient way to cope with this is control of thinking which sometimes can be quite forceful. We literally pause to interrupt the mind's dwelling. We urge the mind to change the focus and straightaway put things in perspective.

5. 3. Negativity Gets in the Way

We will pay attention to negative beliefs later but now we should know that some beliefs undermine psychological wellbeing. They weaken our strengths and they enlarge our weaknesses. Negative thinking gets in the way of happiness. It grows from the negative default of the mind.

Let's Do It Now

Review personal positive statements:

- I am deliberately choosing good thoughts about myself.
- Daily I read this because it teaches me how to control my mind.
- When I feel fear I stop what I am doing and write down when and why I feel it.
- My best friend is not perfect but I get emotional support from them.
- I stop when I feel overwhelmed and do relaxation breathing.
- I maintain optimistic attitude by changing my beliefs.
- Step-by-step I improve self-acceptance. Every day I repeat I'm who I am.
- I build awareness of my negative emotions by writing down their triggers.
- Currently I can't afford doing it and I am okay with it.
- My big challenge is to recognize constructive criticism. I am improving by non-judgemental listening.

Did you notice that previous statements are not only positive but also they empower? Think about possible statements that could generate good feelings and empower you while still considering limits or weaknesses.

My Journal

In this practice you will reflect how the negative default of your mind shapes relationships and personal life. Notice significant relationships including the challenging ones. Don't be afraid, honestly admit your position in difficult relationships. Recognize how current relationships positively or negatively affect your life. Try to connect with your feelings and thinking and write about your awareness.

Personal life: partners, relatives, friends

Work: co-workers, supervisors

Negative feelings and emotions:

Negative mental habits:

6. MIND OVER FEELINGS

"Men are not prisoners of fate, but only prisoners of their own minds."
(F. D. Roosevelt)

Indeed, the mind profoundly generates life experience. Between fifty to seventy thousand thoughts daily occupy our minds. Hundreds of words and phrases, instructions, judgements, assumptions, beliefs create emotionally charged thinking.

We feel good when thinking about something good, and we feel poorly when we think about problems and hardships. The mind is a central lever shifting personal experience.

Illustration

The untrained mind can be illustrated as a puppy, disobedient and wild, the one that needs training. The mind can have unlimited power over us when allowed to run our days. Once we approach it with kindness and love, we become its trainer. Then we turn the mind into a personal power.

6. 1. The Mind's Chatter

Mindfulness, Awareness and Attending

Can you remember your mental conversations, thinking in the form of self-talk that happened a few hours ago? Probably you can't unless something exceptional had happened.

Truly, it's not easy to recall what we think about, remember what we were thinking about a few minutes ago. For that reason we need the awareness.

Monitoring activities in the mind is simply noticing current self-talk, what it targets and how it does it, when we ruminate and mentally dwell.

Content and Ways of Thinking

What we think about creates the content of thoughts. We might target ourselves, beliefs, body, decisions, actions, other people or anything else. The content of thinking impacts how we relate to happenings, other people, their behaviour, the past or future, interpret life events or relationships with the world. People can think about anything and everything. The content of thinking varies enormously.

Depending on how self-talks influence feelings they can be pleasant or harmful, improve feelings or make us feel worse. They can inspire good decisions or lead to sabotaging actions. They help move forward or holdback.

The other important aspect of thinking is the way of thinking. We can advance thorough positive, rational, constructive, encouraging or optimistic thinking. Negative, dysfunctional, critical, unnecessary, sceptical or irrational thinking creates problems.

Stop and Think

Think about the last time you watched a television programme and how it affected your feelings. If you watched the news you probably didn't laugh much, and didn't perceive happiness around the world. If you watched a comedy programme you felt the exact opposite.

Why did the programmes impact you in certain ways? It's because in the mind you were involved in the programmes and they developed your thinking. Thinking influenced feelings. Your mind's involvement resulted in how you were feeling. Perhaps it influenced your further mental conversation, brought attention to something that affected what you have done in response. In response to the mind's chatters targeting ourselves, people or life, very similar reactions develop as when watching a film.

The mind, controlled or uninhibited, is influential, thoughts precede feelings and we can improve feelings with changes in the mind.

Because it is almost impossible to retrace past thoughts and it is relatively easy to catch the current thoughts, we monitor current thoughts and notice present mental activities.

We might start when we are alone, engaged in monotonous or mindless activities such as waiting, walking, being stuck in a traffic. Awareness is paying attention to the content and type of thoughts, recognising how thinking generates feelings and what we do in response.

Our goal is to identify so called patterns of thinking that closely relate to the mind's default. It is thinking run by an automatic pilot, types of thoughts that appear first, suddenly or spontaneously. Because they are run by the default they mostly have negative charge.

6. 2. The Way of Thinking

The way of thinking, often unnoticed, can be run automatically. We might habitually consider that what we think is the truth. Automatic thoughts, significantly affecting our feelings, develop into patterns. We might be unaware of them but they don't appear in the mind by pure chance. The patterns of thinking develop under the conditions and in the environment where we grow up and where we live.

Thinking patterns, in the past considered almost unchangeable, are hardwired in the brain. Fortunately, the brain can adjust and we can literally hardwire them out. Even people who have tendencies to think negatively can change their thinking patterns.

Easy to Say Hard to Do

It is not simple and easy but it can be done once we know how to do it. We need awareness and understanding of our patterns of thinking. Patterns of thinking relate to our development, when we create control and focus of thinking, when as children we receive reinforcement from adults and peers. During personal history we learn morals and values. We judge not only actions but also thoughts. We filter unacceptable thoughts out.

This moral based self-control is central in every society and it halts wrongful actions. The secretive world of the mind, however, still may retain troublesome thoughts, maybe silly, embarrassing, unethical, illogical, senseless, irrational, etc. Problems with self-judgement start when it goes wrong. When we might fail to distinguish thoughts from actions and assess thoughts as facts. We might be too harsh, lack self-understanding, don't reflect actions or we don't justify thinking.

Wrongful self-judgements can grow into big challenges. They can create rejections, faulty self-perception; make us fearful, angry, jealous or inadequate. Judgements induce emotions and false judgements can compromise emotional wellbeing.

Stop and Think

Think about the content of your thinking, what occupies your mind and how you think. What kind of thoughts can you identify when your mind targets you? What aspects of your life you aim at when you are negative? Notice when your thoughts are positive, critical, commending, sceptical, dysfunctional, rational, constructive, encouraging.

My Journal

Situation # 1: You see an old friend walking on the other side of a busy street. You stop and call their name. They seem to notice you and even slow down looking towards you. However, they don't stop, and instead looking ahead they rush away. Answer:

- Why do you think your old friend didn't stop?
- Describe what would you think about the old friend, how would you feel and what you would do.

Once you write your answers read situation # 2.

Situation # 2: A month later, you happen to see the same old friend (from situation # 1). This time they respond, genuinely smile and say how pleased they are at seeing you. You start chatting and they mention that they've been having difficult times. They feel excruciated since their loving partner had a terrible accident a few weeks ago and they feel lost in their tragedy.

Write and answer: What would you think about the old friend this time? How would you feel and what would you do?

Once you are done think again about the situation #1 and #2. Consider the facts from both situations. Rethink and write reasons why they probably didn't stop the first time.

Review your answers and notice if and how the new circumstances affected your interpretation, thinking, feelings, actions and overall experience. Did you interpret their behaviour differently under the new circumstances? If you didn't meet them again perhaps you would feel about them based on your bias thinking the first time. Maybe you'd be convinced about your rightness. Maybe you'd be convinced about your feelings and truthfulness.

My Journal

In your words reflect how the mind can lead to wrong conclusions, decisions, choices and actions.

Helpful Hints

We can observe almost self-hypnotic spells when we dwell on certain mind's chatters resulting in choices and actions. This is well used by athletes, marketing, sales, management or performing arts. They deliberately tap into the minds of people to manipulate their thinking, generate desired feelings and modify their behaviours. That's precisely what you want to do to yourself, functionally train the mind to break old habits and generate the new experience.

We have no reasons to doubt that thinking and beliefs can be intentionally used to trigger wanted feelings and choices.

6. 3. The Mind Lost in Feelings

We are complex beings and sometimes emotional reactions are not direct responses to what we experience but rather to the mind's chatters. We might be lost in uncontrolled thinking that triggers feelings and consequently behaviour. With self-control we can increase predictability of what we feel.

Illustration

When anguish gets worse we speak out thoughts which should be screened out, wrongly act on misjudged ideas or we might completely lose insight. We might go through emotional actions, escalating conflicts or agony. Once in a while this can happen to anybody and we can deal with it. We use other mechanisms to get over it such as forgiving, forgetting, moving on. At times, however, it is difficult, especially when the emotion lasts long or consequences are hurtful.

Improve Feelings through the Mind

Allowing mistakes, forgiveness, self-reflection and letting go are necessary. Somehow we do it but sometimes we fail to be kind and gentle to ourselves. We might struggle with self-compassion or kindness as we limit ourselves by our own thinking and feelings. We become too harsh, too critical, less tolerant when judging ourselves and personal life.

We are emotionally prejudiced, bound by emotional experiences, and the negativity attacking ourselves can be resistant to change. We should remember this and double our effort to change the self-destructive mind.

We have to allow kindness and stop ignoring that we are worthy of the same measures as others. Deliberately develop compassion and gentleness, acknowledge self-values and the importance of positive personal experience. Sometimes the high costs of mistakes maintain guilt and blame. We might be in "a punishment mode", targeting oneself but we need forgiveness to prevent the worse becoming the worst.

Living in guilt or blame is the mind's negative default. It feeds additional dysfunctional thinking making feelings even worse. We should think of guilt as feedback, a reminder we've done something wrong. We should learn and improve our future directions, be better managers of thinking and actions in the future, not to dwell in guilt or blame.

Our ability to forgive is a beautiful quality in us, positive vibration bringing lightness to ourselves and those around us. When we deserve but don't receive forgiveness from others we can deliver it to ourselves.

Forgiveness powerfully counteracts the negative default of the mind.

6. 4. Can You Be Sabotaged by Your Mind?

We are prone to believe that our thoughts are true. Sometimes we fail to assess their accuracy and we let the mind mislead us.

Thinking about ourselves is important in respect to self-esteem because it generates feelings about a person we are. In thinking we value ourselves, have expectations and develop a self-image. Thus the mind's chatter targeting ourselves can positively or negatively impact personal experience.

The mind can become self-destructive and troublesome beliefs can be barriers to accept limits or recognise boundaries. We should be aware of it, train the mind to preserve good thoughts about oneself and personal life. This helps to increase positive experience. We can identify problematic thinking about oneself and personal life:

- Unfair self-criticism: It is often unwarranted and blocks objective reflection of limits, weaknesses, mistakes or flaws.

- Unfiltered criticism from others: It ignores that people use subjective values to judge us and they project their attributes or challenges on others. Unstrained one-sided criticism and unfair criticism.

- Misinterpretations of comments of others: It doesn't recognise compliments or neutral comments and interprets them as ambiguous criticism.

- Disregard or quickly forget compliments: It values negative more than positive or disregards compliments completely.

- Negative beliefs: They measure neutral events as failures or catastrophic mistakes.

- Credits for successes are attributed to luck, ease, inadequacy of competition, to others, or overlooking personal inputs.

- Self-worthiness through comparison with others or possessions: Be less unworthy because others are or do better, because they possess something we don't have.

- Fear of failure, rejection or disappointment.

- Guilt, being ashamed of mistakes, weaknesses or failures and rejection to be open about them.

- Stretched conformity; being bound by judgements of others, disintegrated from personal values.

My Journal

Review the previous points and write about your self-destructive mind. Focus on patterns of thinking when you judge yourself and personal life, self-esteem and feelings about yourself.

7. UNDERSTAND YOUR MIND

The problematic mind can work like lenses that distort good vision. Once they are removed the vision is clearer and we might see what we couldn't see before.

We can start by removing the distortion from the mind, fixing the negative default, and building up balanced thinking. Then we notice the things we overlooked and start relating to ourselves in a new way.

The distorted or problematic minds are

- uncontrolled minds, busy with unnecessary, useless, non-constructive, inflexible, dysfunctional, harmful, judgemental, critical all overly negative thoughts.
- the minds that fixate on the erroneous.
- behind self-induced negativity, anger, fear, jealousy, frustration or low self-esteem.

They frequently fall into some of the following groups of thoughts:

Group	Examples of self-talk and thoughts
• the minds that attack self-esteem	I always screw up; I acted like an idiot; I am a failure
• the minds that avoid letting go	I shouldn't have done it; If you didn't go there you could be happy; I shouldn't have told them
• the minds that lock problems	He will leave me if I tell him the truth; I already wasted all those years so there is no point of changing now; I am not trying anymore; I tried everything but nothing works
• the minds that negatively impact relationships	He never considers my emotions; I am not compromising, They should know better; He has to know how I feel; I agreed but I will ignore their decision

Let's Do It Now

Review the previous chart and examples of problematic thoughts bellow. Think how they might influence feelings, improve a situation or resolve a problem. Think about their quality, impact on relationships, motivation, action and attitude.

Examples of problematic thoughts: I have tried everything and nothing works. I am never successful. I am not able to do anything. I can't do anything right. I have been an outsider since high school. If he wants to be with me he should do what I want.

My Journal

Write few notes about your beliefs and ways of thinking.

7. 1. Development of Patterns of Thinking

Perhaps we all know people who we consider positive, negative, naysayers or inspirers. We can recognize their patterns of thinking and actions. We might consider them pessimists, optimists, fighters, explorers, analysts, victims, givers, drama queens, etc.

We all develop thinking patterns in so called associations, conditioning and reinforcement we receive throughout life.

When we understand how we develop our thinking we can better identify the patterns of our behaviour. We can be curious about negative emotional experience and negative beliefs. Problematic ways of thinking develop in unhappiness, mistreatment, harm, unjustified criticism, negligence or humiliation. We should know how the personal past shaped the mind, what patterns we have developed. Then we should try to change and consciously reframe the mind to develop more functional patterns of thinking.

Stop and Think

Childhood impacts the ways of thinking, beliefs and the way we react to the world; we learn how to relate to ourselves and others. If we want to improve we can fix the wrong ways of thinking and correct the false beliefs. Spend few minutes thinking about your childhood, what and who affected your beliefs and thinking.

Recognise the Dysfunctional Patterns

1. **All or nothing** – the problematic mind evaluates situations as completely good or bad. This type of thinking escalates when something goes wrong or if situations repeat. Things might be looked at in absolute terms or one bad event might be seen as everything goes wrong. These thinking patterns paralyze actions which are seen as useless or waste.

Examples: I can't do anything right. I destroyed everything. I am the only one who is asked to do it. I failed my diet so it doesn't matter what I eat now. It's only me who suffers.

2. **Using judgement erroneously** – filtering out what might be beneficial, dwelling on the negative and ignoring the positive; pick a single negative detail and stay with it exclusively and seeing everything else through a negative perspective, magnifying the bad, minimizing the good, or missing a bigger picture.

Examples: My diabetes ruins my life. I know my boss hates me since she gave me low points in my work evaluation. If they liked me, they would care. I am screwed, everything goes wrong.

3. **Jumping to conclusions, irrational thinking** – Failing to elaborate, investigate facts or ignoring reasonable context as to why something goes wrong. Knowing and basing on assumptions or feelings and reading the minds of others. Interpreting situations without a deeper search for the truth or wrongly predicting how badly things will turn out. Acting as a fortune-teller based on beliefs and avoiding beneficial actions.

Examples: He will never forget it. She didn't have to say it. I know what's in her head. She doesn't have a chance to make it. It will turn against them. I knew you wouldn't get a good review.

4. **Using emotions for reasoning and labelling** – Fail to distinguish emotions, miss rational judgement of one's thoughts and lack of con-

structive assessment. Judgements, opinions or interpretations come from feelings. Emotions are used as facts, evidence for reasoning; they are overstated, incorrectly evaluated and validated.

Examples: It must be me who will be fired. I am hopeless. I feel betrayed. I can't tell him the truth because he won't handle it. I am a loser. I feel like everybody uses me.

5. **Should or shouldn't statements** with no constructive suggestions, blame, dwelling, ruminating, gossiping, criticizing or denying accountability, limits or control. Something happened, it can't be reversed but mentally a person doesn't accept it. The context of what contributes to a problem or situation might be unnoticed. The boundaries might be ignored or existing limits not recognized. Morals and justification might be projected on others, ignoring that other people have different views, thoughts, independent choices, or take their own actions.

Examples: She should have known better. I should always be happy. She shouldn't have the right to do it. He shouldn't feel angry. I shouldn't have been punished. All these bad things shouldn't have happened. If I hadn't stopped going to church he would be with me. I am being punished for my mistakes.

7. 2. What Fires Together Wires Together

We can change the problematic mind if we want. Doing it we need knowledge, stop using the wrong ways of thinking, the mental habits causing harm. We know that what in the brain fires together wires together. That's why the thinking patterns can develop in the first place. To change the mind we have to consciously practise the functional ways of thinking. The brain can respond and adjust. Over time the brain changes. It hardwires in that which we use. Thus, if we stop thinking negatively and think constructively the brain can wire in a new pattern of thinking. It lets changes happen by themselves once we practise these mental habits. Overtime the new way of thinking can become our automatic way of thinking.

Helpful Hints

Have you ever met a person saying they have always been the same? Can it be the truth? Some people probably find comfort in seeing themselves unchangeable; however, we all change through life. Perhaps we don't change the way we might want to because we don't work with the mind. We let the mind's default do it for us. If we want to improve and experience positive changes we have to hold the reins of the mind.

My Journal

Review each paragraph with questions. The questions should navigate your thinking about childhood, the present, and problem solving. Based on the answers write about your ways of thinking and how you respond to life and others. This practice is to increase self-knowledge.

Questions:

Childhood: Was your childhood happy or...? How did you feel about yourself in childhood? How does your childhood affect how feel about yourself these days? What self-beliefs did you develop? Who had the major influence on the way you think and react to life? Think about their thinking patterns and compare them with yours.

Present: Who has impact on your thinking? Compare their ways of thinking with yours. In what ways do you think similarly? Can you recognize their patterns of thinking and reactions to life? Can you recognize yours?

Problem solving: How do you cope with challenges? How good are you in problem resolving? How well are you able to move on, forgive, learn from mistakes and get started? Do you dwell on problems or difficulties? Do you believe in unfortunate fate and if so how does it manifest in your life? How do you value other people? How efficiently do you respond to difficult people? What kind of relationships do you maintain?

My Journal

Review the dysfunctional patterns in the previous section. Copy the following chart. Write two examples of your problematic thoughts in each group and complete the chart.

Problematic patterns:	Impact on your feelings, motivation, attitudes, problem resolving and relationships:
All or nothing	
Mental filter	
Jumping to conclusions	
Emotional reasoning and labelling	
Should, shouldn't, blame others and self-blame	

My Journal

The next practice is to understand what and who the problematic patterns target. Often the harmful mental habits focus on certain things or people. You want to know if there is a hidden agenda behind your mental dwelling. Some people might catch problematic self-esteem, unresolved issues, fear, insecurity, etc. Write in your journal about the content of your problematic thoughts.

You can try to identify contents of: judgements, criticism, rumination, doubt, fear, fixation on past, future, specific people, conflicts or relationships.

8. STRENGTH IN EMOTIONS

Oscar Wilde in the words of Dorian Gray said, "I don't want to be at the mercy of my emotions. I want to use them, to enjoy them, and to dominate them". Did he know that emotions, pleasant or painful, good or bad, shape our lives?

Emotions, may be misunderstood, are engraved in human experience. They are inherent sides of us and they make us who we are; we are bound to feel. Emotions are vital ingredients of life framing our lives, plans, expectations, projections, connections with others. They determine how we interpret the past, present and future.

Perhaps we fixate on the materialistic world while missing something very substantial; we don't attend to the personal inner world that accompanies us at all times.

Emotions are part of us and understanding them can move us towards fulfilment and happiness. We want to start thinking about emotions in terms of their values. They can provide feedback of what has been sent out but we should know the reasons behind feelings. With the understanding of feelings we gain knowledge about what is beneficial or harmful.

Stop and Think

Suppose that something good happened to you today: you won the lottery, were asked on a date by someone you really like, received promotion at work, or anything else. You would feel happy but why? Why would certain things make you happy while others would make you less happy?

Don't Be Stressed about Feelings

In the past and because of religious so called duality, people believed emotions were experiences of souls as rewards or punishments. These days we know emotions are complex experiences. Myths and stigma about emotions might limit our courage to connect with them. We might consider emotions erroneous. We might be too oblivious or judgemental about feelings. Sometimes we don't know what to do with feelings.

Based on personal emotional history, positive and negative, we develop emotional prejudice. This influences our thinking, how we interpret or what we allow ourselves to think. We also have defence mechanisms that we use to cope with difficult emotions. We don't like dealing with our own feelings and we project them onto others.

8. 1. What Do We Know?

We should remember that feelings and emotions can be experienced as reactions to external or internal stimuli; to something happening outside of us or something within us.

Emotions are Different than Moods

Emotions are quite short and intense states and moods can be seen as prevailed emotions. Emotions manifest in moods, usually milder states than emotions but longer lasting. We might not be able to identify triggers of moods, however, when pinning down emotions their triggers can be caught.

Emotions are universal which means a number of basic emotions like fear, disgust, anger, surprise, happiness or sadness, are experienced by people around the world. At the same time emotions are subjective and unique to individuals. This means that the same situation can trigger different emotional reactions in different people. We can experience a range of emotions, variety and intensity or mixed emotions.

Some people think negative emotions are wrong and they should avoid them. It is because negative emotions can be painful and we don't like pain. We might worry that once painful emotions start they won't end but that's not the truth. Emotions are temporary states meaning they start and end. We might re-experience emotions especially those bottled-up.

We can try to handle emotions with emotional management, efficiently process and vent emotions.

Emotional management is based on self-regulation to prevent the return of emotions. When we don't process, we deny or suppress emotions, they intensify and become baggage we must carry. Emotional management is the opposite: we try to understand, allow emotions, feel and let them go. With this we can improve emotional resilience.

For whatever reasons people don't think that feelings can have meanings. As the matter of fact, emotions could be pillars of self-knowledge and self-improvement. They can be remarkable source of recognizing what goes right or wrong. They can guide away from the harmful and towards the beneficial. They can indicate the right things or they can pinpoint what is getting out of balance.

When talking about emotions we have to consider their materialistic aspects which are the processes in the body where the brain plays a leading role. Biologically emotions can be seen as a chain of super-fast reactions when brain and neural system around the body fire multiple signals. These cause changes in hormonal secretion, breathing, blood flow, perspiration and other organic changes that are experienced as feelings. To simplify we can say the brain acts like a super-computer performing numerous activities. It is a simultaneous work of the brain, mind and body at extreme speed.

We should recognize three crucial components of emotions: subjective experience, bodily sensation and behavioural response. Understanding them is a key to understanding how the mind can be involved in emotional management.

8. 2. Three Components of Emotions

Bodily sensations are the most obvious components of emotions. Some of them are subtle, while others are more noticeable like changes in heartbeat, blushing or turning pale, fast or slowed breathing, increased perspiration, etc. Less apparent and more subtle are changes in gastrointestinal activities or glands.

Behavioural response is quite clear and easily observed. It is what we do in response to feelings. It can be any kind of action we do.

Emotions as subjective experiences relate to appraisals. Very simply explained, the subjective experience is a personal judgement of how a situation meets our expectations and goals.

Positive emotions result from appraisal that goals are being met. Negative emotions result from appraisal that goals and expectations are not being met.

Stop and Think

Think about a role of the mind in these appraisals. Most probably it is the mind that provides appraisals. The mind "decides" that the goals are being met, thus we should feel pleasant emotions. It also decides that the goals are not being met and we should feel negative emotions. The mind has "storage of information" that is used in these appraisals. If that's the case shouldn't we modify incorrect information in the mind? Shouldn't we try to deliberately "feed this storage" with goals?

Let's Do It Now

Think about when you felt sadness, fear or happiness. For each try to acknowledge three different components:

- bodily sensation and what possibly happened in your body. Notice changes in breathing, blood flow, muscle stiffness or relaxation, shaky hands, perspiration, etc.
- behavioural responses and what you did when you felt those emotions.
- subjective experience. Sadness and fear resulted from the appraisals that situations didn't meet expectations and goals. Happiness means the opposite. Perhaps you can identify what in the mind caused your feelings.

My Journal

Be creative and playful in this writing and try to improve your understanding of how your mind influences emotions. You might use the answers to the following questions. Why when certain things happen would you feel happy, fearful or sad? What kind of criteria would your mind use to appraise a situation meeting your goals or not meeting them? What possible goals and expectations you might have? How could your mind know what emotions you should feel? Can you specify what in your mind could trigger sadness, happiness or fear?

THE STRONGEST YOU

9. TOWARDS HAPPINESS

The mind can be seen as a judge appraising personal experiences to determine what feelings we should feel.

The mind stores all sorts of information about us such as desires, preferences, ambitions, pleasures, satisfactions, disappointments, successes, failures, wishes, longings, hurts, cravings, likes, needs, rejections, worries, etc. These create a hidden store of information that the mind uses in appraising whether situations meet our goals or not.

Helpful Hints

We have a variety of goals and expectations. Sometimes we are aware of them, other times they are less apparent, hidden or not recognized. If someone feels happy when getting a work promotion perhaps their mind identifies their goals and expectations related to career, ambitions, power or money. If someone feels happy by being invited on a date their goals might be obvious: reciprocation of their feeling. The goals might be concealed like satisfaction of needs, attention, belonging, recognition or intimacy. They might be happy even they don't share their feelings.

The mind can be profoundly involved in triggering feelings and this brings attention to self-knowledge. Once we know ourselves we can better identify the triggers of feelings, then we can better regulate and use the mind to trigger the desired feelings.

My Journal

Write a brief paragraph about your feelings in the last week. Try to find the reasons behind your feelings. Can you identify why your mind appraised situations as meeting or not meeting your expectations? Can you pinpoint the goals in relation to these feelings?

9. 1. Self-Reflection to Improve Feelings

Emotions have social aspects and their expression is loaded with consequences. From childhood to adulthood we develop personal history, emotional prejudice and a level of emotional awareness and regulation.

Societies are equipped with social control to teach their members what feelings are acceptable or how to express them. Social environment carves how we should feel.

Social normalization is important, beneficial and necessary; however, it has dark sides. In a way norms and standards force people to cover and mask feelings in order to fit into society and feel accepted. Religions, cultures and genders also play important roles in emotional regulation and expression. Some people can grow into emotionally immature adults, lack emotional awareness, have underdeveloped self-regulation, struggle with the reading of emotions, they can't sympathize or empathize.

We should be aware what social norms and standards influence how we regulate and express emotions. Mostly we try to feel safe and we are willing to suppress or hide what we feel. Regardless, we should be aware when emotions stay unprocessed. Let's use anger to illustrate.

Anger is a part of so called stress response, fight-flight-freeze-response. It is when the part of the brain called amygdala is active and the brain fires reactions. Stress response is coded in developmentally older parts of the brain we share with our ancestors. Let's say more primate parts of the brain. A body gears up to physically respond and deal with danger as in prehistoric time. Stress response causes an adrenaline rush, flooding with adrenaline and cortisol. Anger harshly disrupts normal functions and we can experience rapid heartbeat, shallow breath, feeling flushed, shaky or tensed muscles, less coherent thinking, being irrational, noticeable changes in speech, increased urge to act-out, fight, yell, hit, throw or hurt. Consequently the body uses homeostasis, natural mechanism to rebalance, get back to normality. We don't have full understanding of how damaging frequent stress response can be but we already know it has debilitating effects on the body and its functions.

Here is the point. To suppress anger is almost impossible but we can do a lot to prevent it when we know what in the mind triggers it. The mind appraises a situation as dangerous, as not meeting goals and expectations. When we feel angry we should subsequently use self-reflection to identify what and why a situation causes it, what false or real danger we are dealing with. This kind of self-reflection is helpful not only when feeling angry but also when we cope with other negative emotions.

Helpful Hints

Emotional management doesn't have to be as difficult as it might sound when we understand the mind, our expectations or what we aspire or desire.

9. 2. Avoidance of Negative Emotions

We may have a habit of avoiding negative emotions. We might associate them with negative events or people, we wish to forget and emotions might be reminders. Avoidance can be an effective, short-term help, a quick fix, and we must remember avoidance doesn't solve. It doesn't remove a cause of bad feelings.

Avoiding feelings as a permanent attitude is troublesome. We might attempt to banish bad feelings but it just doesn't work. Feelings return and become a mind trap urging us to dodge. Impeding undesired emotions is stressful, intensifying other and more complex feelings. Avoidance of negative emotions requires endless vigilance and perpetually activates a stress response.

It's wiser to allow feelings, face them and on reflect them. Negative emotions can be red flags telling us something needs attention. Their avoidance can be rejecting the truth which can't help. Feelings posed by denying the truth are obstructive and stressful. Recognizing the truth can be painful in the short terms but it can be valuable for advancement. Knowing the truth can remove illusions, prevents future disappointments, stops self-blindfolding, acknowledge that something doesn't work well and has to be resolved.

Illustration

Suppressed emotions are like a snowball rolling down a steep snow covered hill. As it rolls it becomes larger and rolls faster. When emotions snowball they become more complex and difficult to resolve.

When we develop emotional management we cope with emotions as they occur. It's like holding the snowball and controlling its motion.

Stop and Think

When someone says their partner makes them angry or jealous, what does it really mean? What kind of attention do their feelings require? To understand should they focus on their partner or their own expectations and goals, in another words should they question if their partner meets their criteria? Always when we want to progress and resolve a problem we should start with ourselves. It requires self-knowledge and we must acknowledge the truth.

9. 3. What Can We Do?

There are two equally important and necessary aspects of emotional management: information brought by emotions and processing of emotions. We have to deal with both. To do it there is a variety of techniques included in this book. Sometimes we can burn the stress response brought by negative emotions in physical activities like running or jogging. Other times we can mindfully attend the feelings, give them space, let them grow and experience them to their end. We can vent the feelings through mental techniques, breathing techniques and release an adrenaline rush without harming ourselves or others.

Working with informational values of emotions requires rationality, thinking with an open mind and willingness to acknowledge a problem. We should be candid and put emotions in a bigger picture in relations to expectations, standards, beliefs, needs, goals, emotional prejudice and limits. Self-reflection should identify what goals and expectations are not met when experiencing negative emotions. See oneself with desires, needs and aspirations, there could be a tendency to project feelings on others or deny the truth. Mindful and non-judgemental attendance to feelings can bring 'aha' moments.

My Journal

Think of one real situation that triggered negative, emotions sadness, anger or fear. To understand the informational value of your feelings try to identify their meanings, your goals and expectations. You aim to healthily (perhaps not painfully) experience unpleasant feelings and burn the stress response. The following questions can help:

What was the issue? Who was involved? What do you think and feel about them? Where did it happen? How were you feeling before and after? Can you notice a hidden agenda or unresolved past issues? How, when and why did this situation start? How did you express your feelings and thoughts? How did the situation end? What consequences did it have? What meanings your feelings had? What did your feelings point out? What did you do to vent your feelings? What would you do differently in the future? What would you do next time to vent your emotions? How can you use the information given by feelings?

Describe what you should do or maybe will do in the future and healthily manage negative emotions.

THE STRONGEST YOU

10. SELF-ESTEEM AND SELF-COMPASSION

When growing up nobody teaches us to differentiate the beneficial mental habits from those that harm. We don't learn in what fashion we can use the mind to powerfully generating positive self-perception.

Within the mind we develop "a unit" of mental habits that relate to ourselves. These mental activities, self-talks, thinking and beliefs target ourselves and personal life. The problematic mental habits such as dwelling, criticism, victimization, rumination, pondering or even daydreaming can have destructive impacts on feelings, motivation or relationships. They activate a wrong mechanism that keeps away from potential to change. They maintain the status quo, negative thinking and feel poorly about ourselves. The negative default of the mind grows within the limitation we put on ourselves.

We want to enter this "unit" and regulate what is going on there. We want to cultivate favourable mental habits and create a new mindset allowing change. The beneficial mental activities not only improve feelings but they also govern healthy choices. They remove limits. They allow seeing one as important, powerful and with capacities to change. Positive self-perception is not only thinking well about oneself but also delivering good feelings.

There are many things in the way of developing positive perception such as personal history, emotional bias, unresolved issues, failures, disappointments, rejections, frustrations, betrayals or hurts. All these unintentionally reinforce the negative mind, consequently deforming self-perception.

Emotional Roller Coaster Up

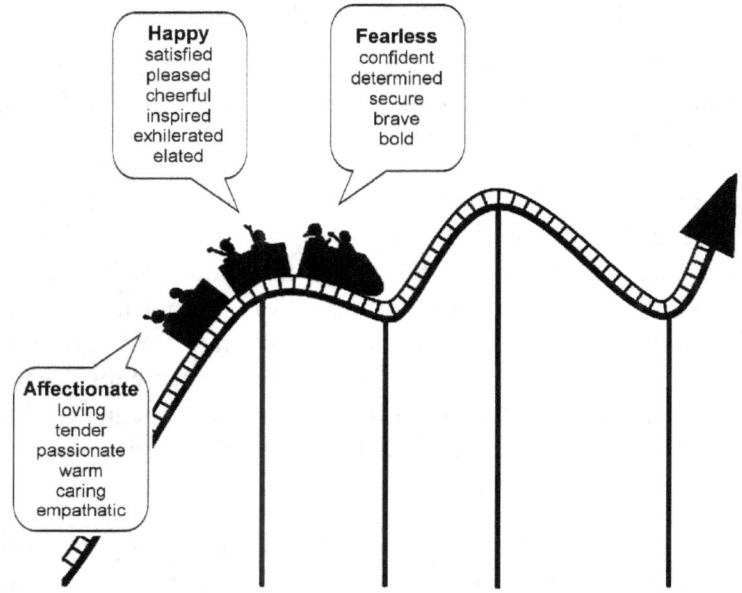

Emotional Roller Coaster Down

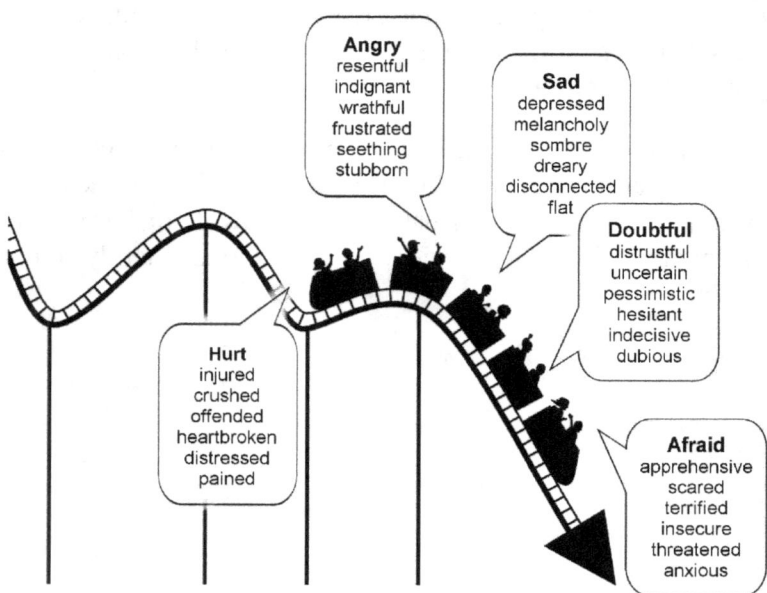

Personal Projection Wheel

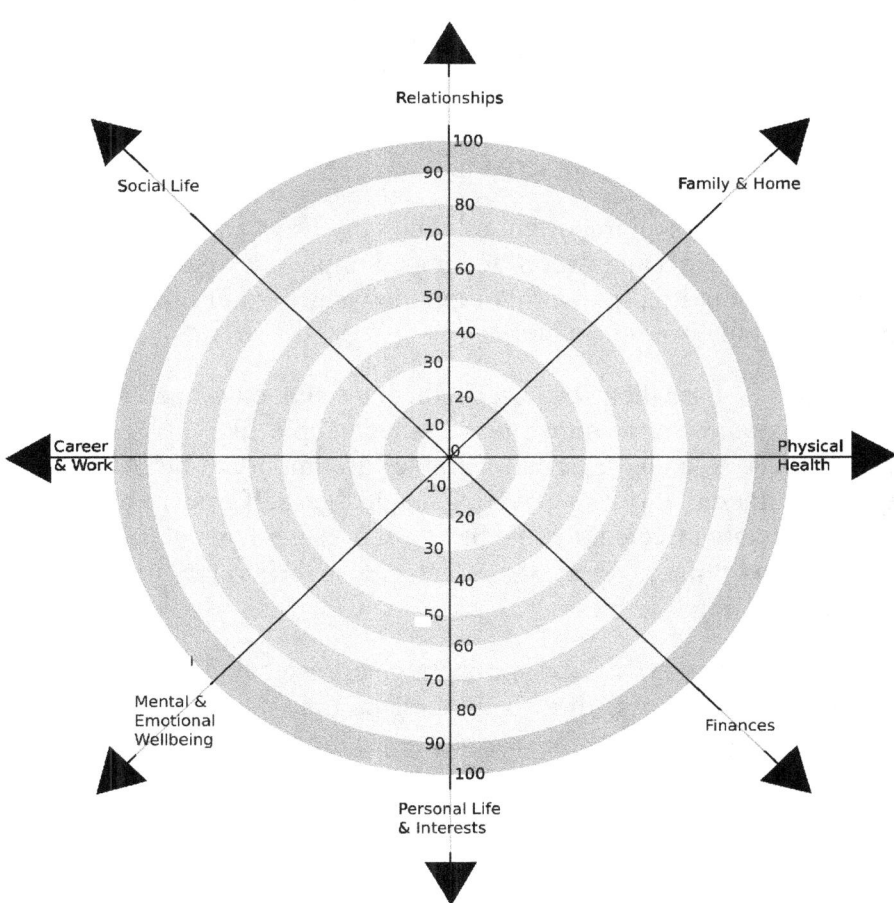

My Journal

Use the Emotional Roller-Coasters and reflect on thinking and feeling about yourself. Think about situations, people, circumstances, your goals or expectations. Can you identify how well or poorly you think and feel about yourself? Use the Personal Projection Wheel and in each area try to identify your feelings.

10. 1. Good Thoughts about You

Self-esteem plays an important role in many ways and it can't be separated from beliefs and overall feelings. Simply put we can't think and feel good about life, the world or others when we don't think and feel good about the person we are.

Many people base their self-esteem on external factors such as money, wealth, physical appearance or whether people like and appreciate them. These so called external variables are important but make self-esteem vulnerable. If these factors change then self-esteem built upon them is widely affected. People basing self-esteem on external factors risk their worthiness. When these factors lose their values these people can start feeling worthless.

There are also internal factors affecting self-esteem. They grow from acceptance, kindness, thoughtfulness, compassion and gentleness. These qualities can grow into a genuinely caring attitude, thinking well and feeling good about oneself. They feed a healthy self-esteem. Healthy self-esteem comes from taking an inventory of a personal reservoir of strengths and qualities as a human being.

The negative mind's default doesn't help towards self-esteem. It can be profoundly imprinted in the way how we think about ourselves. We should elaborate on how twisted our self-esteem might be. We want to develop peaceful feelings about ourselves, accept who we are, what we have to offer the world. With healthy self-esteem we develop respect and awareness of strengths. Do not deny weaknesses or flaws but rather challenge ourself to improve.

We can reprogram the mind through fixing distorted self-esteem. Stop attacking ourselves in negativity and hardwire it out. Replace the harmful mental habits with beneficial ways of thinking. The more we do it, the stronger the circuits in the brain grow. We want to develop positive self-image and self-expectations. They are huge things influencing what we hold onto.

Helpful Hints

It is not easy to accept mistakes and flaws, to be okay with one's limitations, but we have to work on it. There's always someone better than us at certain things. It shouldn't make us feel inadequate, insecure or arrogant. We can put aside comparisons and create healthy self-esteem by identifying values and strengths within ourselves. We want to change if our self-esteem depends on external factors. We should intentionally create healthy self-esteem based on the qualities and strengths we possess.

Let's Do It Now

What are the things about yourself you are grateful for? Try to recognize your strengths or good human qualities. Choose one. Think about it until you feel good, appreciate and have gratitude for this quality. Spend as much time as you need to do it. This practice is to show that focus of thinking can shift your feelings.

My Journal

Review the list of characteristic and relate them to yourself. Mindfully try to identify how strong or weak your characteristics might be. This practice is to bring attention to aspects that are components of healthy self-esteem. In the future you want to embrace the qualities. Copy the ruler into your journal and measure each characteristic by placing it on the ruler:

- acceptance, respect, reliance, control, confidence, worth, discipline, help, improvement, love, protection, preservation, assurance, expression, examination, importance, awareness, satisfaction.

- approval, criticism, pity, hatred, denial.

Ruler

1	2	3	4	5	6	7	8	9	10

Let's Do It Now

Take a moment and bring attention to three things that you like about yourself, qualities you possess, good things you do. If you struggle think what a caring friend might say. Close your eyes and focus on these three qualities. Play in the mind with good thoughts related to these qualities. Try to be grateful for them. Your goal is to trigger good feelings, pleasant sensations in your body. Once these feelings are developed, savour them for few minutes. If you wish, write in your journal about your experience.

10. 2. Why Self-Compassion?

When seeing things we don't like we tend to be emotionally reactive and things get worse. It's like instead of be kind to someone after making mistakes we hurt them and make them feel even worse. This is what we frequently do to ourselves.

Self-compassion can be seen as the opposite of self-criticism which can come from well-meanings or as motivation to do better. We are self-critical because we don't want to fail, make or repeat mistakes. We also want to protect others, be better and we might think that self-criticism is what we need.

Truthfully we need to recognize the wrongful then put attention and energy to change. Dysfunctional and hurtful criticism and self-criticism are pointless. They come from the mind's negative default. They activate a stress response harming the body.

We need self-compassion to heal and release negativity. Instead of criticism, beating ourselves up for wrong doing we need gentleness. We should train the mind to notice and forgive. We can savour the beautiful human qualities we possess. With their cultivation we become more caring, allow seeing the previously overlooked things within ourselves.

Perhaps we notice that it is difficult to appreciate ourselves or might struggle to acknowledge the good within us. The resistance to self-appreciation reduces with conscious practise. Then the mind and brain by themselves respond and improve. Our task is to do it, give them the chance and apply compassion, kindness, gentleness and savouring. This is the mind's reprogramming. We shift the focus of thinking to fix the negative default. The good thoughts reflect in positive feelings. Compassion, kindness, gentleness and savouring feeling pleasant. They are uplifting experiences and we shouldn't deprive ourselves of them.

My Journal

Write about self-compassion, kindness, savouring and gentleness, why and how you can develop them.

THE STRONGEST YOU

11. LEARN TO LIVE WITH THE PAST

Wouldn't it be nice if the brain and mind preserve only cherishing stories and not the painful personal past? If emotions were only reactions to current experience and not brought by memories?

People can hide incredible stories behind their face, sometimes painful and unforgettable. Life would be easier without the aching burden of hurts, disappointments, betrayals, regrets, frustrations, let-downs or losses. Unfortunately, as humans we don't have much choice and frequently agonizing hurts stay with us for years. Their effects last long into adulthood, sometimes even into the late decades of life.

When in a study people were exposed to negative and positive experiences they remembered seven times more detail from negative ones. Perhaps by default the mind holds on to aching stories. Bad memories can feel almost in the whole body, in every cell, feelings, senses and energy as the past is carried on. We can use a deliberate effort and focus to reverse this; learn to live happily regardless of the past.

Throughout life we somehow learn to cope with the hurtful past but we don't always do it to our wellbeing. When the past aches we might disregard, deny, reject and feel ashamed, angry or jealous. Indeed we should heal the upsetting past and live in peace with it. Personal stories ask for acknowledgment, understanding, acceptance, forgiveness, compassion, gentleness and kindness.

Emotional and mental pain is a part of human experience. Perhaps, there is no person in the world who wouldn't know it. Yet nobody teaches us how to cope with it until we hit the bottom line. If the psychological wounds are serious, limit our functioning, if they incapacitate us, we should find professional help. Sometimes we might be embarrassed to admit we need help. We might wait until we become dysfunctional and can't get pain out of our system. We should seek help and end suffering long before we hit the bottom. We don't want to make things worse than they are. Opening past wounds might be frightening and indeed painful. We should wisely judge if we are able to handle it on our own.

Old hurts are like carrying a heavy sack, a sack which becomes heavier after each hurt. It pushes us down. We keep dragging it regardless of its weight. We might feel exhausted and perhaps this is the time to open it and start removing the things. As we do it its weight changes and gradually we can straighten up. The move forward can be lighter when we let go of past hurts.

11. 1. Are Memories Changeable?

Similarly to a filing cabinet that stores files, our memory is organized in files. When we pull a file from this system it brings memory and emotions attached to it. Files from a filing cabinet can be modified or destroyed, and in the similar way we can do it with memory files. With some imagination we can destroy bad files, rewrite files, and modify the content and emotions related to them.

Memories are thoughts about the past. We tend to trust and believe them but there is trouble with memories. They are not reliable and the negative default of the mind makes them selective.

We should know that cognitive psychologists who study the accuracy of memory want us to be alert. They try to understand how emotional memories behave in the remembering process and research how we encode past stories, store them and then retrieve them.

Psychological studies suggest we should be cautious when trusting memories. Their findings point to the inaccuracy of memory. Our memories change by the act of recalling them. This might be surprising but recalling a memory every so often makes it less accurate.

Every story we preserve in memory is shaped by the times we have recollected it before.

We should be aware the brain and mind can betray us, transform memories every time we bring them to our attention. Does this give more reasons to stop dwelling or ruminating on aching stories? We can intentionally pull memory files into awareness and modify them. When we bring files up we must remember it's the past and not us as we are today.

Reconciliation with the past can't start by suppressing emotions. It's the other way: allowing feelings, recognizing the truthfulness of feelings, acknowledging the right to feel, non-judgementally relating to them. Treat them like a loving mother would attend to a wound of their child.

Emotional reconciliation can be built with the use of the mind. We should deliver compassion, kindness, acceptance and forgiveness. We can even be bold and change the interpretation of personal stories. We can mindfully change our fixation in them, find meanings, learn and move on.

11. 2. Personal Story and Feeling Good

We can make life easier by removing from the mind all the unnecessary stuff we hold onto. We should do it to make space in the mind for new thoughts that will generate desired feelings. It is us who can allow it to happen, acknowledge the things that are harmful are not necessary and work on their reprocessing. The past is gone and beyond current reality. It is retained by mental habits and we can permit ourselves to let them go.

We can shift our focus from the past to the now. Put the past in a bigger picture and see it from a wider view. Turn attention to the things that matter these days, accept those already gone. We should think about the personal past as something that we experienced and we don't have to hold onto. Deal with the consequences of the past and look ahead. The goal is to reset the mind's focus and change the emotional attachments to past wounds.

Change is possible whatever past stories we carry on. It is the matter of how we think about them. We have to permit ourselves to let go of the past, accept, create inner peace and reconcile. Thinking matters a great deal. If we want to improve feelings about the past we have to regulate how we think about it. We should deal with what we probably never liked and let it go. Accept the feelings coming with it and never dwell on it. We shouldn't be afraid of feelings as they start because they will end. We might need time and courage. Sometimes just allowing the feeling means we feel better. We should bring kindness, understanding, gentleness and compassion to reconciliation with the past. The liberation from painful feelings can't be based on hate, anger, blame or guilt. Once we allow good thoughts the feeling shifts.

Helpful Hints

Unresolved feelings grow bigger and their intensity can become unbearable if we neglect them. If we continue stuffing ourselves with negativity about what is over, we don't have space for improvement. We can think about the capacity of a glass and what happens when it overflows. Similarly, we all have limits. Being bitter about something from the past creates personal suffering. While keeping painful memories vivid we feel the pain, not the people behind them. The past is as it is. We should permit ourselves to let it be.

Let's Do It Now

Painful memories might from time-to-time pop into the mind, triggering unwanted feelings. Some can relate to childhood, parents, guardians, teachers or friends. Some might be recent when we were mistreated by others, coworkers or bosses. We might feel sorry, pity, angry or poorly about what happened. When we resist the awful feelings and try to defend against them, we make it worse. The feelings will return and they might feel stronger, grow more complex.

My Journal

Think about your painful stories that might need reconciliation. Try to think why you should deal with the unresolved (maybe sooner or later it will creep on you). Take notes in the journal about them. Prioritize the issues. Write what you will do to reconcile them.

11. 3. Leaving the Past with Compassion

Probably emotional hurts are more frequent than physical, yet people oddly react to them with rejections or criticism. They don't treat them as they would treat physical hurts. As untreated wounds can get inflamed, ignored psychological hurts can grow tender.

We deserve self-respect, appreciation, gentleness, kindness, and instead of self-criticism we should nurture compassion. Through mindfulness and mental practise we can start new relationships with ourselves and others. We can deliberately cultivate compassion to ourselves, become kinder and gentler. We might resist but doing this is crucial. If not for anything else we should do it to have a pleasant uplifting experience. With regular practise the positive feelings deepen and increasingly they become the mind's default, hardwired in the brain.

Helpful Hints

Aching memories might feed negative beliefs often grown into fears, doubts and loss of hope. We might fear that because we already suffer, the misery will continue or it won't change. This can create desperation, a trap of pity or victimization. Treacherous feelings can be signs that we don't correctly use the mind. Probably we don't think in peace, don't accept, ignore limits or we fail to adapt. We should use the energy and regulate thinking and beliefs to absorb a positive attitude.

My Journal

Choose one thing from the past that you would like to change your feelings about. Answer: Why would you bring respect, acceptance, compassion, gentleness, kindness and forgiveness into this issue? What benefits and costs would it have?

11. 4. Mental Anticipation of Good or Bad

We all mentally anticipate how well or poorly things work for us. What meanings we find when something happens to us. What we expect from ourselves and for ourselves. What we believe we deserve to receive. We have self-expectations and self-perception. At large they are how we perceive and interpret personal experience in relation to ourselves. There is a close relationship between them and our emotional past. When holding onto painful old stories we can hardly maintain positive self-expectations or self-perception.

Some people hold negative images of themselves resulting from past rejections, disappointments, abuse, fears and other negative experiences. Some people don't expect that good things can happen to them.

They might perceive themselves as those who always loose, fail, can't achieve, etc. They have negative self-expectations and self-perception.

Other people can see brighter sides of whatever happens to them. Mentally they anticipate good turns apart from their aching experience. They expect the good things to happen to anyone including themselves. They preserve positive beliefs and firm mindset. They have positive self-expectations and self-perception.

These two opposite types of people have dissimilar experience based on how they interpret the past events. They uphold mental anticipation and therefore they allow positive or negative reaction to what happens to them. They have different self-images developed on expectations and perception.

Examples of negative self-image with low expectations & negative perception:

They will make fun of me. I am not going there. I know I will fail. They always reject me. I have the same fate as my mother. There is nothing good for me. I am always picked on. I can't find a better partner. I won't find happiness. I am cursed. I never try, there's no point. My fate is to suffer. It runs in my family. Bad things will happen to me as the last time. I won't be able to get through these difficulties.

Examples of positive self-image, positive expectations & perception:

Even though I was fired I can find a good job. My father was an alcoholic but it doesn't mean my partner will be. I lost my temper many times and I can stop doing it. I failed to lose weight and can succeed this time. Losing my job forced me to take the college program. Look what good that loss brought to me. I don't understand why this happens but I know I can handle it. I am alone and I can enjoy it. Sometime I will have a soul-mate. I went bankrupt and I am recovering. I can overcome these difficulties. Even it hurts I am strong to go through this. My last failure made me stronger.

Helpful Hints

Interpretation of why bad things happen influences our expectation, focus, goals, motivation, actions or choices. If we believe we deserve hardships and difficulties we will experience them. Whatever life brings we can't avoid experiencing hardships and difficulties. Contrary, if we are able to find positive aspects in hardships and difficulties, we experience them with ease. We even might learn and effortlessly move forward. A negative mental anticipation can be a huge barrier to advancement.

Stop and Think

Think about your mental anticipations and self-image. What do you expect from and for yourself? How do you interpret negative experiences, past difficulties, negative stories? How do you interpret all positive things that happens to you? What type of future do you expect for yourself? Can you identify beliefs that maintain positive and negative self-expectations and self-perception?

My Journal

Review previous examples of negative and positive self-image to help your thinking. Write ten realistic and positive self-beliefs that you wish to have. Read them aloud. How do they sound? What do you feel when you review them? What would you have to do to personalize them? What good would you get if you identify yourself with them? Write your thoughts and answer the questions.

THE STRONGEST YOU

12. DON'T TRUST TO YOUR BELIEFS

Mental systems consist of organized items of knowledge, images, ideas, assumptions and beliefs. We understate beliefs and their roles in mental and emotional functioning. They profoundly impact personal happiness and satisfaction.

Beliefs Are Not Feelings

Sometimes beliefs are referred to as feelings of knowing something, but that is wrong. Beliefs are thoughts, starting as principles they grow into convictions and regulations. They are the thoughts creating the whole scheme of the so called belief system.

Beliefs are strong authoritative thoughts anchoring personal judgements, decisions, choices and actions. They guide how we interpret, understand, what meanings and values we find or what purposes we can identify. Beliefs are normal, all people hold some beliefs. We should also know that beliefs are rigid and inflexible thoughts. We can see them as the inner law we follow. We should know what beliefs we maintain because we can't act against them. If we preserve false and wrong beliefs we might unintentionally limit ourselves.

12. 1. Understanding Beliefs

We should elaborate our beliefs to acknowledge the functions and meanings beliefs play in our life. There is a high chance we might hold onto false beliefs that comprise emotional wellbeing, acting as wrong filters. We would expect that rational thinking screens out false beliefs and we let them go. Unfortunately, this is not always the case. At times we preserve wrong beliefs because they somehow work in our mental functioning. We might not recognize them or don't see their incapacitating impacts. How can this possibly happen? It relates to the brain and attachments people create.

The brain builds connections that we experience as attachments. We might be attached to people, animals, objects, places and ideas. Beliefs are ideas and when developing them we create connections with them, emotional attachments. They can be experienced as aversion or affection. We become affected by what we believe is correct. We feel emotional aversion to what we believe is wrong.

Beliefs are not whatever kind of thoughts. They have strong emotional dimensions. We like what we believe in and dislike what we don't believe in. This explains why we might maintain false beliefs or be wrongfully convinced.

We must know that when we believe in something we commit to it. We want to be compatible with beliefs. When we think or feel in conflicts with beliefs we suffer because we see it as wrong. Once we believe in something, whether our belief is false or true, we still commit to it. If we want to change false beliefs it is helpful to know how they develop to begin with.

In childhood we create "just the world beliefs". Those are the simplified beliefs helping children socialize and understand the world. In "just the world beliefs" everything in the world is good or bad, the things happen as rewards and punishments. Because adults want offspring to believe in a predictable world and feel safe they teach them this simplicity. They want children to believe that when they do well they will be rewarded, that good things happen to good people and bad things to bad people, that nice things are good, etc. "Just the world beliefs" work well with children and children leave them behind when they better understand the world.

As we grow we adjust false beliefs similarly as we stop believing in fairy-tales. We learn the world is more complex, punishments and rewards are indirect, good people suffer, fairness might be scarce, not everything nice is good, and so on. Before we grow into adults we should have fairly well adjusted beliefs according to knowledge and age. Indeed, mostly this happens but because of emotional attachments when developing beliefs we might fail to adjust some. We should thoroughly review self-beliefs because we have strong emotional attachments to them. It could easily happen that until adulthood we might hold onto false self-beliefs.

12. 2. Beliefs about Yourself

We all believe something about ourselves, skills, capacities, abilities, limits, values, talents, strengths or weaknesses. These beliefs we base on our past experiences and this might be a problem. More or less we develop self-beliefs in childhood. When we personalize ideas of others, identify ourselves with what others reinforced. Core self-beliefs can reflect the values other people saw in us, what they supported in a child we were. They can be results of how other people conditioned our thinking. Our emotional attachments could be based on what was planted in us, regardless it's true or false. Later negative experiences could make our false beliefs stronger and emotional attachments deeper. We really should be aware of false beliefs and work on their adjustments.

Helpful Hints

A common belief, "I am not good enough", children bring into adulthood. People might not see them false or resist changing them. When rationally thinking about the meaning of this belief we must find its nonsense. What does it really mean to be good? How much is good enough? How do we measure goodness? How do we know when we are good enough and start thinking we are good enough? Who are we comparing to?

This is an example of dysfunctional and false belief developed in conditioning and reinforcement. Such a belief is irrational and probably has strong emotional attachments. A person who beliefs this might struggle for most of their life or unless this false belief will be replaced by a functional belief.

12. 3. False Self-Beliefs

The negative default of the mind and troublesome life experience could strengthen false self-beliefs. We can develop the awareness of self-beliefs any time and try to adjust the beliefs that hold us back. We really don't have to be stuck with self-beliefs such as those making us unequal or inadequate. We should be willing to replace them with rational beliefs. Because we know the beliefs could mirror ideas of people who shaped us we want to be sure they are not false. We should let go of false beliefs and create the ones reflecting what we prioritize. Beliefs should reflect current values, good feelings, capacities we possess, abilities we see in ourselves, and potential we wish to reinforce. With the use of the mind and techniques we can restructure the belief system.

Stop and Think

Review examples in the following table. This is to illustrate how we can approach beliefs to know their functions and possible attachments. Think about how this example might talk to you.

Note: New balanced belief is what we wish to develop.

Belief:	"I am not good enough"
Feelings:	Feeling inadequate, belittled, unworthy, unaccepted, unsatisfied, ambitious, jealous or insecure
Source:	Childhood and youth – pressure to prove importance & conditionally accepted: probably achievements stayed unnoticed or spoken unimportant, reminded accomplishments could be better, told other do better, comparison with others, inadequacy was pointed out
Advantages:	Tendencies to try the best, more or harder than expected. Feeling accepted, good and worthy when in success or when acknowledged. Self-esteem grows in achievement or in recognition.
Disadvantages:	Conditional self-esteem: achievements only briefly improve self-esteem. Reversing feelings according to emotional attachments. Taking very hard when unsuccessful. Failures reinforce emotional attachments.
Effects:	Difficulties to freely relate to others. Projection of negative emotions. Misinterpretation of actions and word. Possible insecurity, self-belittling, defense, jealousy, competition.
New balanced belief:	"I am worthy the way I am."

My Journal

Copy and complete the following table. Analyse one negative self-belief. Once you do it memorize the new belief. Remember to repeat it frequently. Each time when you notice the old belief immediately replace it with the new one. Continue doing it until you forget the old one.

Belief:	
Feelings:	
Source:	
Advantages:	
Disadvantages:	
Effects:	
New balanced belief:	

Stop and Think

Think about people from your past who influenced development of your self-beliefs, perhaps you internalized their ideas. It might be family, religious groups, members of community, peers, friends, teachers, media, etc. Bring attention to a negative self-belief. Think about the aspects in the blank chart: feelings, source, advantages, disadvantages and effects. Answer: Is this belief true? What in your experience supports and what contradicts this belief? How do you interpret situations that contradict this belief? How does this belief impact your self-image? Why is this belief important? What would a loving friend (a person who cares about you) say convincing you this belief is false? What would be a new balanced belief replacing it?

My Journal

Choose another negative self-belief you would like to change. Use the chart from the previous page and complete the table. Memorize the new belief to replace the old one.

Stop and Think

Review other examples of negative beliefs. Perhaps they remind you of some of yours. Think about the impact of these beliefs. How do they influence decisions, choices, people you choose, things you do? Try to identify personal beliefs that might compromise self-esteem, expectations and how you feel about yourself.

Examples of negative and false beliefs:

- I don't deserve better
- I got it from my mom
- I can't get along with people
- I have to make others happy
- Whatever I do, it never works
- I am a failure
- I always have to please others
- I never do it right

Let's Do It Now

Review the table and fill in the possible feelings and emotions:

Beliefs	Emotions / Feelings
I don't deserve better	
I got it from my mom	
I can't get along with people	
I never do it right	
I have to make others happy	
I am a failure	
I always have to please others	

Compare your answers:

Beliefs	Emotions / Feelings
I don't deserve better	Sad, resentful, sombre
I got it from my mom	Powerlessness, pessimistic, helpless
I can't get along with people	Inadequate, worthless, dejected, alone, hurt
I never do it right	Sad, self-rejected, sceptical, weak
I have to make others happy	Stressed, worry, unsatisfied, disappointed, dubious, hesitant
I am a failure	Contemptuousness, irritated, annoyed, bitter
I always have to please others	Self-dismissal, inadequate, upset, hurt

Examples of negative thoughts:

Thoughts	Emotions / Feelings
Something is wrong with me when I am not happy	Sad, dismal, depressed
I never get use to these people	Fearful, alone, worry
My fantasy is embarrassing	Ashamed, inadequate, humiliated
This will never work for me	Hopeless, weak, paralyzed, sceptical
I have to lie to be accepted	Downcast, upset, distressed
I would be fired if they know I am on medication	Fearful, afraid, alarmed, panicky, inadequate

The next task is to learn how we can develop balanced thinking. Balanced thinking should include realistic beliefs that reflect personal values. If we can't develop positive beliefs we should be neutral and truthful which can still be empowering. When modifying the way of thinking we always consider emotional attachments this can generate.

My Journal

The following practice has multiple steps and you shouldn't rush with it. This important work is to guide how you can correct negative or false beliefs. As the first step use the Personal Projection Wheel to identify one negative self-belief in each area. This way you will list eight different negative beliefs.

Personal Projection Wheel

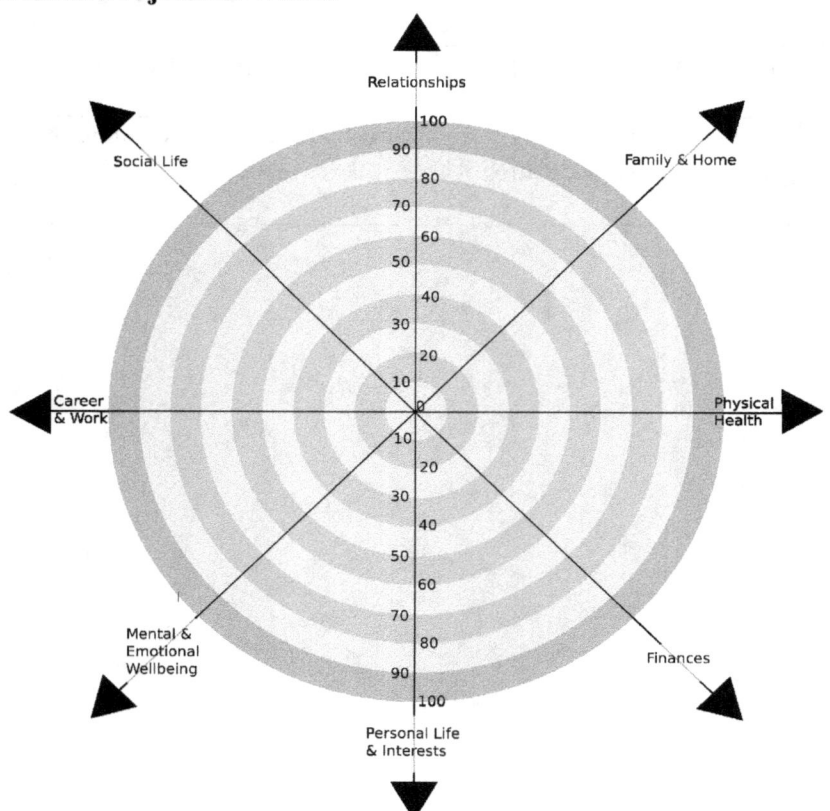

My eight negative beliefs I want to change:

...

...

...

Then copy and complete the following table for each belief. This way you will create and fill in eight tables.

Belief:	
Feelings:	
Source	
Advantages:	
Disadvantages:	
Effects:	
New balanced belief:	

Make a list of eight new balanced beliefs as you determined in the tables.

My new beliefs:

...

...

...

Copy the following chart and in the cells write new beliefs. Identify emotions and feelings in the second column. Next, rate the importance of new beliefs on the scale 1-10: 1 is low importance and 10 is the highest importance.

New balanced beliefs	Emotions / Feelings generated by new beliefs	Priority of new beliefs (1-10)

Your next task is to choose a belief with the highest importance. Memorize the new belief and repeat it frequently. Each time when you remember the old belief immediately replace it with the new one. You can write the new belief on an index card, use mobile devices, computer screen or paste it somewhere you can often see it. Continue working with your beliefs based on their priorities.

Note: This way you can work with any dysfunctional thoughts or beliefs. With practise this will become easier and you won't need a written format. The written format is necessary to learn. In practise your skill grows.

Changing eight different beliefs can take some time. You are encouraged to do it on your own in the future. Now it's time to move to the next chapter.

THE STRONGEST YOU

13. DEVELOP THE POWERFUL SELF-IMAGE

It's staggering that we can identify desires, the things we would love to do or experience and mostly we leave them behind. Not many people turn their plans into actions, do what satisfies them, achieve what gives them fulfilment and meaning. Why does this happen? Are we more prone to fail than succeed? The answers reside in the mind and its negative default. People who follow their plans take a different route than the majority. They use the powerful mind, learn and advance.

13. 1. Impact of Self-Image

Many factors play roles in personal achievements such as personality, attitude, emotions, circumstances, interpretation of successes and failures, motivation or coping with obstacles. However, there is something more important, maybe the least obvious, positive beliefs and self-image. They grow upon courage and trust that we are able to turn potential to success, that we can utilize necessary skills to achieve. In other words, if we believe in ourselves we have positive feelings and expectations. We create empowering beliefs that we can act upon, and we do. This kind of self-image is built upon strong self-efficacy, the powerful positive self-image manifesting in actions and achievements.

Before we examine our self-image and how strong a self-efficacy we possess we will playfully use imagination and try to project personal future, unleash fantasy to have rough ideas about what we desire and want if everything goes well.

Let's Do It Now

Imagine yourself one year from now, once everything goes right. Think about your current needs, plans, wishes or goals and use the following questions to help: Where do you live – place, city, country? What do you do – school, work, fun, social life? Who are important people influencing your life – family, friends, co-workers, or others? What makes you happy? What do you do to feel good? What do you do to be healthy?

My Journal

Write the date one year from today and title "My Personal Projection". Write about what you imagine could happen in a year from now. Once you are done, do the same to project personal future in five and lastly ten years from now.

Five years from now: Where do you live – place, city, country? What do you do – school, work, fun, social life? Who are important people influencing your life – family, friends, co-workers, or others? What makes you happy? What do you do to feel good? What do you do to be healthy?

Ten years from now: Where do you live – place, city, country? What do you do – school, work, fun, social life? Who are important people influencing your life – family, friends, co-workers, or others? What makes you happy? What do you do to feel good? What do you do to be healthy?

Is our self-image positive or negative? Do we possess strong efficacy? As a matter of fact the answers are not as vital as our willingness to improve. We want to strengthen self-efficacy and gradually create a positive self-image. Before doing so we should know where we are standing at. It is helpful to identify characteristics of strong self-efficacy and reflect what we possess or lack.

Characteristics of strong self-efficacy:

- Seeing challenging problems as tasks to overcome and take actions
- Focus on process and activities not only on the results
- Strong sense of commitment to interests or activities
- Recovering quickly from setbacks and disappointments
- Defeating challenging tasks or obstructions
- Strong beliefs in one's ability to cope with difficulties and chal-

lenging circumstances

- Emphasis on the personal strengths
- Maintenance of confidence in personal potential
- Ability to find and utilize necessary resources
- Commitment to create and stick to plans and goals
- Being in charge of decisions
- High awareness of personal influence to the results

My Journal

Review the characteristics of strong self-efficacy and think how they relate to you. Create two lists: 1. Characteristics you currently possess 2. Characteristics you currently don't have or you want to improve.

Let's Do It Now

Review the two lists in your journal. Reflect personal experience, examples from your past achievements or failure. This practice should question how realistically you assessed yourself. You should frankly acknowledge the strengths and weaknesses. If necessary revise your lists. The current self-image is guidance to know what has to be improved.

13. 2. Trust to Feel Good

Self-efficacy can direct towards strengths we want to cultivate with confidence. We want to develop self-believing and trust that we can do or succeed regardless of negative experience. We learn from the past failings or losses, and use confident beliefs to advance. Positive mindset includes courage to face challenges, see difficulties without worries and constructively coping with them. When we adopt a positive mindset we change attitude. We might be like children, maybe playful and flexible. We can start fixating on solutions not the problems, not pondering on hardships rather what we do to change.

Growth of strong self-efficacy is a process. Missing characteristics develop through planning and actions. We can do it with the focused mind and intentional practise. Changing attitude and mindset can prevent giving up in difficulties. We can use personal statements to address weaknesses.

Illustration

A good example of a personal statement might be "I can make things happen when I have the right plans and tools".

Self-beliefs could sound: "I believe in myself", "I follow the plan", "My willpower is getting stronger", "I don't give up", I am focused", "I can use all available resources", etc.

Gradually, when we replace false and negative self-beliefs we can create a new self-image. A self-image of the person we wish to be: who is focused, does things step-by-step, solves problems, believes in self or allows the changes to happen.

My Journal

Review your list of current characteristics of self-efficacy and create five self-beliefs to strengthen your self-efficacy. To develop these beliefs refer to previous chapters. Create new beliefs, one at a time. Strengthening of self-efficacy is a process. It should be your goal when you finish this book. Now you move to the next practice.

My Journal

Review your projected future in one, five, and ten years. Considering your current conditions realistically think about the future. Use the personal projection wheel and the chart to develop personal goals. Some of them can overlap categories.

Personal Projection Wheel

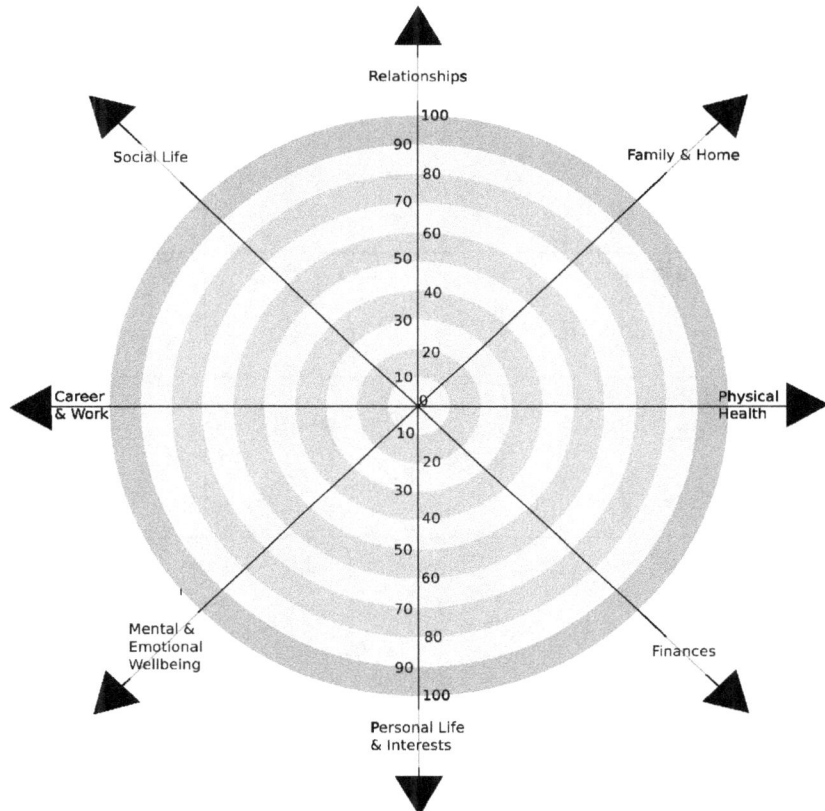

Area	Goals		
	1 year	5 years	10 years
Family and home			
Relationships			
Emotional wellbeing			
Physical health			
Social life			
Career and work			
Interests			
Finances			

13. 3. Happiness from Within You

When asked what would make us happier, we give many answers: greater wealth, a nicer house, vacation, a trip around the world, health, finding a loving soul or having a beautiful family, you name it. We see happiness differently because we have variety of needs, aspirations, expectations, beliefs and morals. We also experience events and losses that influence where we search for the happiness. At times, what was desirable yesterday loses its values today because our needs have been changed.

In the last century American psychologist Abraham Maslow studied human motivation and created a pyramid of needs. His followers have elaborated his theory to better understand how people grow on satisfying needs. They suggest that our needs grow in satisfaction and we are driven when we have meanings. We can use this knowledge and improve. We can try to find meanings, understand the needs and goals.

We naturally know our needs in the same ways as generations before us who were closely connected with themselves. Because of the changes in modern society we live fast stressful lives, we disconnect and relate to ourselves somehow distantly. We might follow others, believe that what makes others happy would make us happy, or we might go through days automatically, not even trying to make our days brighter. It doesn't have to stay like that. We don't have to pass opportunities that would make us happier, miss possibilities that would represent positive changes.

We should stop fixating on what's around us and become aware of what within us matters. When connected with personal life we can react to events that negatively or positively change our fulfilment. We could use the pyramid of needs and personal goals to help. We can develop a personalized pyramid of needs to reflect current priorities and directions. When we develop a hierarchy the meaning of daily actions is transparent.

Pyramid of Needs

13. 4. Positive Reactions to Negative Events

Circumstances always play roles and we can soften impacts of unfortunate events with efficient adaptation and positive responses. Instead of dwelling on misfortune we can choose an empowering approach; copying and adjusting. We know that people can thrive in unfortunate situations while others can be miserable in fortune. The empowering approach is the matter of focus. It is the meanings we choose to hold in any kind of circumstances.

Dr. Viktor Frankl, Austrian neurologist and psychiatrist who survived the Holocaust, referred to prisoners' reactions not as a mark of the conditions but also as the freedom of choice. According to him the prisoners had freedom of choice to hope, find meanings, not to disappoint themselves, their loved ones or God. Once we lose the freedom of choice we lose hopes and probably we give up.

Maybe we all know someone who seems always to be taking the right steps, getting out of misfortune. We can assume that their coping mechanism is highly efficient. They are well grounded in their life, know themselves. They probably well understand that it is not what happens to them that matters as much as what they do with it. We don't choose losses and often they catch us by surprise. It is easier to cope with them effectively when we stay well connected with personal life and needs. When we have meanings they guide our daily actions.

Let's Do It Now

Consider someone you know and who is well connected with themselves, probably beneficially respond to life, understand and satisfy their needs to advance. Create a clear picture of them. Then think about an opposite person, who appears to be just going through life, maybe complaining, victimising or almost like going in circles of life. Answer the question: What characteristics of theirs do you recognize and why do you see them in one way or the other?

My Journal

Copy a pyramid of needs and try to develop personal hierarchy of current needs. You might want to use the personal projection wheel to help you in identifying the areas of needs.

Personal Projection Wheel

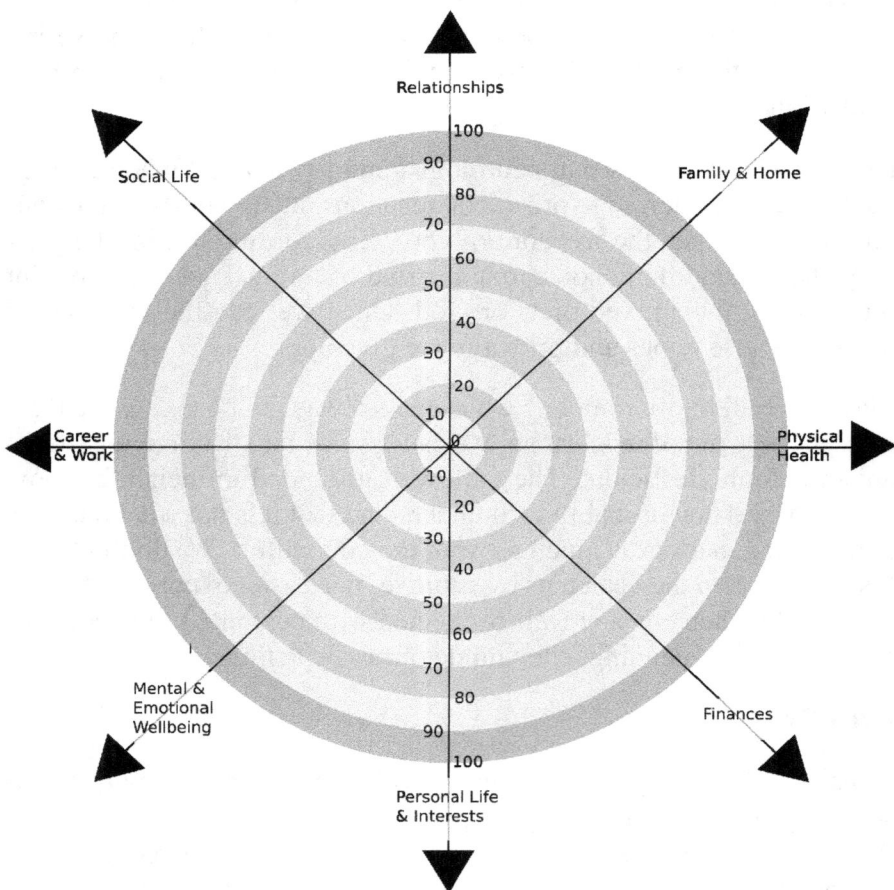

14. CREATE MEANINGS AND GOALS

Perhaps we associate goals with the outside world, areas such as business, career, productivity or finances. Personal goals are not dissimilar and they have higher personal importance. Just as we help our friends by guiding them, personal goals can be our guidance. By having goals we express meanings, intensify focus and determination. They can positively influence life experience. Personal goals say what we want to achieve. They are checkpoints of direction. They can correct when we derive, return us back on our path when drifting away.

As long as we hold the correct targets, remain committed, and perform accordingly, we should be progressing. Personal goals can be a strategy to stop fiddling around, having purpose and meaning of daily actions. Goals can help to regulate the negative mind. In our goals we can target personal improvement. Almost anything can be a subject of goals: mental habits, patterns of thinking, beliefs, feelings, self-image, acceptance, forgiveness, choices, confidence, trust, persistence, determination, values, willpower, relationships, self-esteem, etc.

14. 1. Different Types of Personal Goals

We can use short-term goals to cover the things we want to do within days or months, long-term goals to plan future up to five years, or lifetime goals to reflect philosophy and vital values. Goals should complement each other and harmonize what we want to reach now with what we want in the future. The short-term and small goals could be a strategy to achieving big and long-term goals.

Helpful Hints

When creating goals we should consider our feelings. We should be curious why want to achieve something, what would we feel in the process of achieving, how the goals and the process of achievement would affect people who we care about. We should be interested in emotional reasons behind the goals and achievements.

Stop and Think

Reflect on two personal events: positive which moved you to better places in life, made you happier or overly positively affected life, and negative: the one you wish hadn't happened, you might see it as a mistake, failure or overall its impact was negative. Choose them based on consequences. Think about how much or how little you had planned them. Compare anticipated consequences with actual ones. Think what would be different if you had planned.

Examples of events: leaving an abusive partner, school graduation, marriage, birth of a child, signing a mortgage, walking to work, meeting up with parents on weekends, reunite with a friend, accepting extended responsibility at work, going to therapy, visiting a new dentist, etc.

Illustration

Without personal goals we are like boats sailing on the open sea with no navigation. Navigation makes the journey more predictable and aimed. Personal goals can be our navigation and help us to hit our target. They can state our agenda and be the path to correct choices. They can give meanings to days. Without meanings and direction we can be easy objects for those who have plans and know how to get us where they want us to be.

Nothing is Too Small to Target

We don't want to dwell in negativity of the mundane yet necessary things we don't like but have to do. Those are the little things that could make our days miserable. We can break wrong habits, improve feelings or attitude with the small goals. We can use them develop the right mindset, acceptance, new routines, etc.

We can be creative and playful with small goals. They can target thinking and boost new types of mental habits. The negative mind tends to ruminate on mundane, unfairness, unfortunate circumstances or dwell on problems. With small goals we can develop mindfulness to make ordinary things acceptable or even joyful. With small goals we can better cope with difficulties and replace negativity with positive approach.

Illustration

Training the mind with daily goals is simple and empowering. Examples of small goals might be: "Today I will appreciate myself for these three things: _," Each time when washing hands I will repeat this positive belief: _."

Helpful Hints

With small goals we can change attitude and mindset. When incorporating a positive approach the feelings shift. Positive approach motivates powerful actions. As illustrated in the chart the way we think about an issue and how we interpret it can be influenced by small goals. This way we can gradually develop a positive attitude towards whatever we prefer not to deal with. Small goals can help to move from dwelling to problem resolution.

Negative Approach Run on Automatic Mode	Positive Approach Developed with Small Goals
Thinking This drives me crazy. Why do I have to do this? I wish I never agreed. I can't do this. Other people in the office have time for everything. I am stressed. I worry I won't do it on time. **Feelings** trapped, powerless, desperate, victimised, angry, inadequate, demotivated	**Thinking** I am doing this because I have no other option now. Next time when I will be asked to take extra responsibility I consider my limits. **Feelings** calm, accepted, powerful, motivated, in charge **Goal**: When I have negative thoughts about this issue I immediately correct them.

14. 2. Be Smart

Small goals can gently force the mind to notice other things and target whatever small stuff. We should be using so called smart goals. This is not a new concept and smart stands for:

SMART - Specific, Measurable, Achievable, Timely

Let's Do It Now

Goals can be powerful when correctly developed and used. We want to learn how to create smart goals and distinguish from wrong goals. Review the examples and create three smart goals.

Examples:

I will improve self-esteem.

> Smart goal: In next two weeks each time when I am self-critical I will tell myself, "I am alright with who I am."

I will be better to myself.

> Smart goal: Today I will tell myself three kind words whenever I will see my reflection in the mirror.

I will improve relationship with my brother.

> Smart goal: From now I will say two compliments to my brother each time when I talk to him.

I will feel good about my life.

> Smart goal: Every morning I will spend five minutes practicing gratitude about three things in my life I appreciate and why.

I will be a better daughter.

> Smart goal: I will call my mom twice weekly and drive her to doctor's appointments every month.

I will lose weight.

Smart goal: I will exercise every Monday, Wednesday and Saturday for 15 minutes from today until the end of June.

I will get better marks in Spanish.

Smart goal: I will study Spanish daily for 15 minutes until the end of the course.

I will take care of my sugar intake.

Smart goal: From now on I will stop adding sugar to my tea and coffee.

Illustration

Someone wants to learn to meditate. Starting off with sitting in quietness for fifteen minutes could be unrealistic and unachievable. Probably they would quickly give up, might say meditation doesn't work for them. Smart goals can help them to develop meditation skills. The goals would reflect their limits and abilities. They might start with five minutes sitting to achieve calmness then stretch the time and so on.

Let's Do It Know

Try to create five smart goals to develop meditation skills. The final target is fifteen minutes sitting in quietness.

Keep the Flexible Mind

Correctly set goals should be encouraging, motivating, checking progress and overall helping to achieve. They should allow checking direction and timeline; realistically reflect current conditions and existing limits. We want to divide big goals into parts to experience achievements with less effort and in a shorter time. Too big, vague, unrealistic, or goals relying on external sources are to easily given up, turn into frustrations and disappointments. Goals are written strategy and we should direct attention in the process of achieving and maintain focus in everyday activities in a process of doing. The results are important but the movement towards them is more vital.

We should always consider feelings when creating goals. We don't want to unintentionally target what increases stress or causes conflicts. We should acknowledge costs and decide if they are worthy of sacrifices.

Because of unpredictability we should respond to unplanned surprises that might affect our goals. New circumstances might change our views, priorities and needs might change. We might be forced to reassess goals to improve a situation. Although we create goals with an intention to achieve if necessary we should adjust them. Sometimes we do better when replacing goals than fighting negativity around them.

Helpful Hints

Whether we encounter unexpected situations, meet new people, fall in love, have unforeseen opportunities, we should reflect on them. Some events can move towards achievement of goals, while others may hold us back. Sometimes our plans can totally blow out. We should be aware that once goals lose any of their qualities (of SMART) they stop working.

Stop and Think

Beforehand it is helpful to have a strategy helping to overcome obstacles and difficulties. Think about what possible hold-ups and setbacks you might face. They might grow in current conditions, limits, motivation and overall self-efficacy. Think about personal strategy that would help you to achieve your goals.

My Journal

Copy the chart and create a draft of your smart goals. You can use your personal projection in one, five and ten years you developed few practices ago. On the calendar mark a day in a week you are planning to finish this book. That very day you will review the draft of your goals and finalize them. Refer to previous Stop and Think. Make a list of potential hold-ups. Write what you will do to overcome them.

Area	Goals		
	One year	Five years	Ten years
Family and home			
Relationships			
Emotional we wellbeing			
Physical health			
Social life			
Career and work			
Interests			
Finances			

THE STRONGEST YOU

PART TWO
KEEP PRACTISING
TO BE THE STRONGEST YOU

THE STRONGEST YOU

15. MINDFULLY REDUCE STRESS

A small amount of stress can be motivational, improving performance, resistance and adaptation. Excessive stress, however, grows into many problems and its costs can be dramatic. We should be willing to change otherwise we are unpredictably wearying.

Stress triggers stress response when the brain sends signals of threat and makes a body readily to fight or escape from danger. We experience bodily changes as increased heart rate, changes in breathing and in digestive activities, reactions in endocrine glands and production of hormones. Chronic stress can be dangerous; weakening the body, decreasing its ability to rebalance and causing premature wear down. Stress is behind decreased focus, inability to relax, development of insomnia, conflicts or worsened relationships. When stressed we filter out positive experiences, ruminate in fears or worries, and we maintain negative emotions that over time grow more complex. In pre-disposed individuals stress can trigger development of psychological disorders, clinical depression, anxiety disorders. It increases a chance of psychiatric episodes, schizophrenic or bipolar episodes.

We should know that chronically stressed people are prone to risky and compulsive behaviour. They substitute desired pleasant feelings by wrong choices, finding pleasure in compensatory behaviour, impulsive actions, binge drinking or eating, alcohol and drug abuse or gambling. Chronic stress negatively influences executive functions of the brain, affects cognitive functioning and strengthens dysfunctional thinking patterns. The longer stress lasts the more difficult it is to change or break wrongful habits.

We can learn strategies to cope with and prevent stress. The efficient and long lasting techniques tap into thinking, beliefs, values, mindfulness and acceptance. We can practise weighing the stressors against what's beneficial to the mind, feelings and body, future and relationships.

When we embrace functional thinking we control how we relate to the world, including the stressors. When we maintain a positive attitude towards ourselves we don't allow stressors to compromise wellbeing.

When we understand risks of a chronically stressful life, measure it with the costs of personal wellbeing, we are willing to put the things in a bigger picture and decrease stress.

Unintentionally we might maintain stress by having the wrong approach towards the triggers. We might have incorrect focus. Instead of thinking about the difficulties by themselves we should focus on how to resolve them. This way we regain power, identify what we can do then deal with stressful issues.

We might think about stress, the way it makes us more stressed, thinking how life is stressful, how little we can do to change it, project stress on others, blame others for stress we experience. This attitude takes away our control and intensifies the stress level. We should acknowledge that it is us who allow stress or others to make us stressed. We fix on dark sides, don't accept or don't recognize opportunities for growth and learning.

15. 1. Through the Powerful Mind

Once we stop avoiding stressful situations and deal with them our strengths and control grow bigger. When stress is caused by our wrong decisions we should stop pondering on problems, address whatever is behind prolonged stress and resolve it. It might temporarily increase discomfort but it moves towards improvement.

Stressed people somehow forget to prioritize, wrongly interpret what causes stress and forget being constructive. Once we look at problems by measuring their values with an open mind we can find different views. We might recognize the truth of others or be open to try another approach. We can think what value a problem will have in the future, whether it will really matter next week or next month. Weighing problems can take away frustration and give us a break.

We could be surprised how much we eliminate pressure when we change attitude, preserve positivity and acknowledge limits, power or control. Immediately we can feel release when we stop seeing ourselves as those who must suffer or are victims. In whatever tense situation putting ourselves in a position of free choice instantly improves feelings. We can create written lists of things we do, things we chose to do, things we and others control. We don't have to sweat small stuff. Even if our schedule seems stretched we should value the few minutes we relax. Maybe we have to start noticing and enjoy little things we can still do, or we might proactively do them.

Self-reflection

Another way of reducing stress is to reflect on all the things we do, be grateful and appreciate whatever we have completed. When catching negative thoughts we can immediately replace them with empowering and constructive thoughts. Knowingly we can look at problems with ease, focus on positive, recognize limits and remember that we do as much as we can.

Awareness

There are many activities we do such as walking, driving, travelling or even communicating that tend to run on automatic pilot and default. They can increase tension or we can do them mindfully, attend them fully. We should exercise mindfulness and use mundane things for mental training; remind ourselves that only the present moments matter nothing else.

Helpful Hints

Undesired thinking maintains focus on unwanted circumstances and it doesn't do any good. We can recognize it by words like always, never, should, must, or shouldn't. When feeling fear, anger or sadness the negative mind dwells and ruminates. Immediately we can eliminate misguided thoughts, gently redirect the mind to overlooked aspects.

Acceptance Is Mental Agreement

Some sources of stress are inevitable and if we can't stop them or remove them from life we should change how we regard them. They don't have to be sources of stress. We can recognize them as the reality of current life, make peace with them and accept as they are now.

Acceptance is mental agreement with the present state, with what can't be changed now and might be different in the future. Acknowledging current limits is always easier than railing against them. Actions or decisions of other people can be frustrating but we are not in charge of them. Rather than thinking about them we can focus on the right things, take personal accountability, actions and decisions.

Acceptance of the world full of contrasts, restrictions and conflicts decreases stress levels. People are imperfect and so is the world, making mistakes is normal and letting go of them should be as well. We can choose to attend what matters, create a list of things we currently don't control, face the limits and accept them. Present reality won't last forever. Self-induced stress can grow from exaggerating and seeing problems in places where they are not. They might be just realistic limits. The Buddhists say if there is no solution to a problem, there is no problem. Indeed, if we can't resolve something today, accept it as it is today. Maybe tomorrow we will be wiser, a situation might improve, solutions can appear.

Adaptation to Cope Better

Beliefs might be in the way to adaptation. Dwelling on standards that don't work is self-sabotaging. Adaptation is a useful way of coping with the triggers of stress. It allows regaining power through changing expectations. Perfectionism is an avoidable stressor. Once setting reasonable expectations for ourselves and others we reduce distress. Developing the flexible mind that can compromise is a liberating strategy. We should be willing to change especially, if we expect others to change. Being agreeable and finding middle ground is the way forward.

15. 2. Actions to de-Stress

Behaviour plays a huge role in stress. We should be aware that our wrong behaviour can make stress worse. Sometimes we trap ourselves in self-sabotaging actions and harmful choices. Actions that can profoundly decrease stress level include better organized work, single focus, scheduling, planning and having goals. We shouldn't forget to relax and re-energize even if our schedule is busy. It doesn't need much time and it pays off well.

Plan Beforehand

Proactively designating time for the things that we find enjoyable, make us laugh or bring humour into life, can make significant improvement. Every day doing something little that we enjoy is more revitalising than two week exclusive vacation once in years. If we regularly find time for fun, we are in a better place to handle stressors when they inevitably appear.

When we're stretched too thin or running behind, it's hard to stay calm and focused. Schedule keeps stress levels under control, goals and plans that we stick to allow paring down the to-do-list. We should consistently and often analyse schedules and tasks. We must prioritize, distinguish that which we think we should do and that which we really have to do. Often we consider many things to be important and ponder that all should be done immediately. Give second thoughts, prioritize, drop tasks that aren't truly necessary to the bottom of the list or eliminate them entirely.

Leisure activities interrupt the tense feelings. They don't have to be time consuming and can still bring joy. Include "easing times" on calendar. They can be as little as: watch a favourite show that makes us laugh, write a journal or stories, designate ten minutes to progressive muscle relaxation or meditation, read, dance, sing or listen to favourite music. Intentionally we should build a habit of daily laughter, include laughing at ourselves. Humour in life is necessary. Laughing relaxes the mind and helps the body rejuvenate. We don't consider life too serious or dramatic. Rather look at the funny sides. Life can be a comedy, sometimes a black comedy.

We can greatly improve feelings by self-nurturing, doing little things that boost gentleness, savouring, compassion and self-compassion. During the busy and stressful days we shouldn't neglect emotional self-care, stay grateful for any kindness given to ourselves and others. We shouldn't avoid self-care, procrastinate when other obligations encroach. In advance we can plan the amount of tasks, work and breaks. Regular breaks should be priorities. Temporarily leaving responsibilities behind allows recharging after hard work. Resting and joy are necessary. Giving them little significance is a sign we don't care much about personal wellbeing.

Sometimes talking to other people can be comforting. When we choose the company of others, we should prefer optimistic people who enhance our values. Positive relationships can uplift feelings. A good social support buffers stressful days. We should mindfully choose topics, avoid stressful topics, gossiping, whining, criticising or complaining about the things. We can choose to talk about the things cherishing goodness and positively influence everyday life. If we have an urge of emotional venting we do it with the right people, do it in the right place and at the right time.

Physical activities are critical de-stressors. Energetic movements reprocess the body's stress response and we should do them regularly. Getting the whole body to move and sweat can be anything we enjoy. We can chose what we like if it's dancing, jogging, jumping, aerobic or bike riding.

Regular exercise strengthens the body and mind. It improves sleep, stimulates mental functioning and elevates feelings. Prolonged exercises promote overall wellbeing. They can also act as natural opiates. During vigorous energetic exercise the brain releases chemicals producing good feelings. Chemicals giving good feelings are called endorphins (serotonin, epinephrine and dopamine) and physical exercise can boost their production in the body. They are associated with relaxation, pleasure, optimism or feelings of euphoria.

Quick Fix

Sometimes stress builds so high that at some point we might experience an intense "stress attacks". It might feel like we're going to burst or blow. Ideally the physical release helps but for whatever reason intense exercise that would burn stress response is not possible. Then we can try to quickly decrease stress level. They can abruptly release, interrupt negativity and immediately reduce tension. We should be aware that intense stress attacks can be a red flag.

Quick fixes:

- dip the hands and forearms in cold water, let cold water running down the wrists and forearms, wash face and eyes with cold water, splash face with cold water, rapidly tap around the body with fingertips, strike body or swiftly brush it with fingertips, gently strike the body or swiftly brush the body with hands
- punch pillows, scream into pillows, shout muffled by pillows, jump.

15. 3. Communicate Assertively

Ineffective communication can increase a stress level. Not everyone is good in self-expression. Sometimes we must push ourselves to do it. We have to practise to develop effective self-expression to avoid more difficulties in future. The more we do it the better we become.

We might have difficulties to say what we think, say no when we are asked to do something. We might think rejecting someone's requests or additional tasks would be wrong. We must be well aware of our limits, control how much we take on and express it.

Making ourselves heard in assertive ways empowers, improves one's positions, increases respect and makes relationships transparent. People who suppress self-expression become unconstructive critics, appear cowards, complainers at wrong places and to wrong people. We shouldn't bottle-up opinions rather send assertive messages to the other sides. This reduces stress, overall develops confidence, and moves us to a better place in the long run.

Helpful Hints

Saying "no" and reasoning why "no" might be strange at the beginning but with rehearsals it becomes less difficult. When acknowledging our limits we exercise a respectable way to honestly express rejections. This way we spare ourselves from additional complications. Once accepting unachievable responsibilities it's difficult to explain why we fail to meet them. It is easier to clarify that something is beyond our possibilities than making false promises that we don't keep.

Assertive Self-expression

We want to find comfort in being assertive yet positive. We shouldn't agree to things because we are expected to do so, rather wisely judge decisions beforehand. Assertive communication helps dealing with problems up front. We should actively contribute to relationships; stay grounded and possibly change the dynamic of a relationship through assertive communication. We shouldn't be passive, not caring nor letting others make decisions for us. Passivity can turn against us. We should be aware of one's position in relationships, particularly those stressful or imbalanced, boundaries and powers of everyone involved.

15. 4. Stressful Relationships

Practicing self-expression, saying personal opinions and feelings in an open and respectful way is generally valued. If people don't voice thoughts or feelings courteously, resentment builds and situations likely remain the same, if not worse. Confidence of self-expression builds in practise and gentle pushing oneself to rehearse self-expression is not a bad thing. It pays well down the road, improves positions and personal values in relationships. Also it prevents stress developing due to suppressed thoughts and feelings.

Fear, anger, jealousy or doubts can be controlled by the mind. Genuine expression improves understanding of a relationship, how the parties contribute and what can be changed. Self-expression works as a learning ground to improve and strengthen personal involvement. Overall it reframes inadequate relationships. Through assertive self-expression we can grow respect and self-respect.

Know What We Can Control

A person having troubles with self-esteem always pulls the short end and not just relationships by themselves are problems. Having a problematic self-esteem contributes to stressful and imbalanced relationships. If we don't feel well about ourselves we must change our thinking to improve feelings. There is also a downside of self-expression and we should be compassionate about mistakes. If for whatever reasons things go wrong learn from mistakes and fix the consequences. We can build strategies for the future, let negativity go. Deliberately we should move from pity or bitterness towards resolution to maintain balanced relationships.

In any difficult time we might want to talk to a trusted person and choosing professionals bound by confidentiality is not a bad choice. It allows self-expression, venting suppressed thoughts and feelings. It can be very cathartic and therapeutic; just hearing one's own voice genuinely expressing. Even if there's nothing that can be done to alter a stressful situation it helps.

Sometimes we might struggle with boundaries. The extent of involvement of others in our life and our involvement in lives of others is our choice. Quality of relationships improves once we understand and accept boundaries and limits. We control time spent with others, what we share with them, and also we regulate thinking about them. Intentionally changing the ways of thinking about people who increase our stress will shift our feelings. We can change standards and expectations to eliminate the negative charge. We don't create false images about others when accepting mistakes or limitations. Staying neutral about someone is better than pondering on their flaws. Trying to change others or make them to meet our expectations is unnecessary stress we might create. Our role is to actively and positively contribute. Our verbal responses increase or decrease stress.

Sometimes the most stressful people can be family members, co-workers or bosses. We can't or shouldn't terminate these relationships rather learn how to cope with them efficiently. Topics of conversation are our choices. We don't have to discuss what might increase tension. We have the right to stop or excuse ourselves from uncomfortable conversations. Mindfulness profoundly helps when we have to resolve a problem whit difficult people. Sometimes our own poor choices of words and responses contribute to stressful communication. It is healthy to reflect on them, learn from mistakes and move on. Forgive and decide what can be done differently in future and follow through.

If we are in unequal relationships we should be aware of it because the side in the better position knows it. They know how to pressure or manipulate, make us to do what they want us to do. We need a strategy beforehand and know how to stop them, don't allow this to happen. They might urge quick decisions and sometimes excusing ourselves and gaining time can help.

When we maintain mindfulness and positive attitude communication becomes easier. We resist being reactive or making choices under pressure. We better consider potential consequences, benefits and costs of suppressed expression.

15. 5. Technique to de-Stress: Use Focus

Some days the mind can be preoccupied by too many things. We might lose the ability to prioritize and this increases stress. When we consider too many things important or too many things necessary to be done at the same time we should pause. For a few moments we intentionally redirect focus to something meaningless. Something unimportant and unrelated interrupts all that business in the mind and enambles it to regain focus.

This technique can be used as a proactive de-stressor at different places or times. We use visual focus, single focus that redirects attention to something completely irrelevant, indifferent or new and it works as a distractor of the mind. We choose an object of focus: a jewel, rock, talisman, plant, picture, statue, cup, pen, etc. Some people carry small objects they like a great deal, have some meaning to them or remind of something good. The easiest way is to use a thumb: Stretch the arm and hold the thumb up.

Let's Do It Now

Do this practice while sitting. Fix your sight on the selected object and focus all your attention on it. As you breathe slowly and deeply, hold the sight and full mental focus. Try to notice every little detail of the selected object, intentionally let it occupy your mind and don't allow any other thoughts. If many thoughts return, gently close your eyes to interrupt the focus and keep them closed for a minute. Then open your eyes and start looking at the object again. Fixing the sight and mindfully observing the selected object.

We can do it for two minutes or longer as we might wish. Don't stretch time particularly, if you struggle with focus. The goal is to fully attend to details and bring all thoughts to it. If you practice this technique regularly you can increase time to improve focus.

15. 6. Mindful Breathing to Relax

This easy practice interrupts stress by shifting awareness to breathing. Sit in a chair with closed eyes and do it.

Let's Do It Now

Gently bring attention to your breath. Don't force it, breathe naturally. Let the breath find its own rhythm, gently increasing alertness of your body while breathing. Hold the whole awareness in the moment, not interfering just simply feeling the breath. Notice the entry and exit of the breath as you inhale and exhale. Pay attention to the impact of breathing on your body. Be aware what happens in your nose, mouth, throat, chest, middle stomach cavity, etc. Be present and feel. Be genuinely curious about breath. When noticing your attention has wandered from breath, bring it back and stay interested in breath. Doing this over and over as many times as you might need. Stay gentle, patient, kind and curious about current experience. You can do it for three minutes or longer.

If you like you can start as described and gradually start regulating the breath. Slowly breathing in and breathing out, deepening your breath without force, while staying aware of its effect on your body. You shouldn't force the breath rather gently controlling its speed and depth. Always you notice its effect on the body. If thoughts or feelings arise, just recognize them. Don't suppress them, just try to observe them, and allow the things to happen. Let the thoughts go by redirecting thinking to breath, staying curious about breathing.

To finish, whenever you're ready just allow your eyes to open. The more you practice the better you get.

16. RESET THE MIND

This chapter focuses on self-defeating beliefs and teaches how to modify them. These types of beliefs are barriers to improvement. We might resist recognizing the truth. They block acceptance, adjustments and trust. Sometimes we bargain good feelings for self-serving beliefs. Self-defeating makes us resistant to what might be good for us but because it is in conflict with our beliefs we reject it. Because of destructive self-defeating beliefs we become insecure, self-sabotaging, avoidant, fearful and stressed. We might miss opportunities and be fearful of taking healthy risks. We might worry too much to face challenges which are good for us.

Illustration

Self-defeating beliefs have an overall negative impact. Imagine you believe that you always have to be perfect; whatever you do has to be done one hundred percent. This belief has many advantages: forcing you to work hard, be focused, persistent and determined; you give out more than is required. However, this belief has a lot of disadvantages and it makes you not feel good most of time. Perfectionism conflicts with joy. Perfectionists are driven by results while rarely enjoying what they do. It creates constant stress and frustration.

16. 1. Change Self-Defeating Thinking

We want to be aware of self-defeating thinking. We can identify self-defeating thoughts and self-defeating actions.

Self-defeating thinking is irrational and it can be acknowledged within the patterns of problematic thinking discussed in previous chapters. Self-defeating thinking can relate to: fears, trust, courage, achievements, approvals, attachments, compulsions, blame, entitlement, hopelessness, worthlessness, inferiority, anger, narcissism, conflicts or rejections. Self-defeating thinking might be resistant to change but we can do it.

Examples of self-defeating beliefs:

- I should always control my emotions

- People should be kind
- I am a nice person people should like me
- People should like me because I act for their benefits
- If I am alone I must feel miserable
- What's wrong with me if she rejected me?
- I should never be sad
- I should never feel angry
- I should always be happy
- People should be the way they are expected to be
- I am more worthy because I am a boss
- If I am not loved there is no reason to try
- Nobody would like a flawed person as I am
- I should feel bad when I see my mother alone
- I am less when I don't control my emotions
- If I don't impress people they won't like me
- People are demanding and they have power over me

Self-defeating beliefs are part of personal emotional prejudice. Their emotional attachment means that we often don't pay attention to our thinking. Sometimes it is easier to recognize self-defeating behaviour. Behaviour that helps to compensate perceived or imagined inadequacy is linked to self-defeating thinking. When we notice for example that we avoid or procrastinate we should ask why we do it. We can consequently retrace thinking. Then we can better understand how our own self-defeating thinking manifests in life. The next chart shows how self-defeating can work.

Self-defeating thoughts	Emotions / Feelings	Behaviour
I am wrong when I am sad	Inadequate, depressed, hopeless / headache, teary, stomach pain	Isolation, avoidance, engaging in risky behaviour or substitutes such as medication, drugs, cigarettes, alcohol
I never do the things right	Hurt, fearful, guilty, blame / shaky, muscle tension	Procrastination, avoidance
To feel fear is wrong	Shame, inadequate, embarrassed, / rapid breathing, sweating, lump in throat	Avoidance, risky behaviour, substituting such as medication, drugs, cigarettes, alcohol
Nothing works for me	Hopeless, sceptical, angry / blurry, physical discomfort	Avoidance, procrastination, passive –aggressive leading to conflicts or arguments
I would be fired if they know I am a gay	Fear, ashamed / discomfort in body	Avoidance, withdrawing search for comfort or risky behaviour

Let's Do It Now

Identify five problematic beliefs that you would categorize self-defeating. Then think about emotions and feelings they trigger and maintain. Lastly try to specify behaviour and finish the chart.

Self-defeating thoughts	Emotions / Feelings	Behaviour

16. 2. Costs and Benefits of False Beliefs

As we work with beliefs we try to find the evidence of their truth or falseness. We think rationally to allow noticing what might be wrong. We do it because the mind might resist change unless we examine and get insight. Then we can replace old beliefs with new ones by tapping into the mind and modify beliefs. We use Costs / Benefits sheets to find the evidence.

Self-beliefs can be seen as the story we tell ourselves and now we want to know if the story is correct, change if it is incorrect. Know why the story is wrong and into what we are willing to change it. The art of changing beliefs is to use the mind to develop realistic, emotionally less bias beliefs.

Instead of judging beliefs as right or wrong in terms of morals, we look at their advantages and disadvantages in the ways they influence feelings and wellbeing. What hidden benefits they might provide. We question their impacts on motivation, choices, decisions, behaviour and how they affect our relationships with ourselves and others. We try to see both, good and bad sides. We can use this technique to determine even seemingly innocent self-beliefs.

Review the following chart to understand how we approach beliefs, their costs and benefits.

Belief: I always have to be perfect.	
Costs	**Benefits**
My perfectionism causes me stress and worries. I focus on small details. I can't see the things in a bigger picture. Even small stuff can be overwhelming. I never feel I succeed because I always feel I should do better. When I fail or make a mistake I am devastated. My perfectionism locks my creativity. I can't take healthy risks. I am afraid of failure. I have fear of criticism. I annoy others by being perfect. I try to impress others by accomplishments and this pushes people away. I can't enjoy what I am doing.	I work hard mostly more than others. I feel great when I succeed. I don't accept mediocrity. My high standards show that I'm a special. People think of me as a talented worker. I'm above other people. I don't accept just average results. I feel good about myself when my hard work is rewarded. I am conscientious. People like my high performance. I am a good example appointed by the boss.

Notes
Conditional self-esteem that depends on achievements and recognition, mostly not feeling happy, difficult to build healthy relationships, perhaps hidden jealousy, difficult to accept others, dwelling on small stuff.
Decision: I want to change it.
Reasons: This belief causes me many problems. My partner left and she called me the most annoying person. I don't accept mistakes of others and they avoid me. I like my achievements but don't like myself as whole.

Let's Do It Now

Choose one problematic self-belief and complete the chart. Use the chart for as many beliefs as you want to comfortably work with false beliefs.

Belief:	
Costs	**Benefits**

Notes
Here you will write about your feelings, additional thoughts and problems caused by this belief

Sometimes we might resist changing old beliefs and develop new beliefs. We might need to work on letting go of the resistance at first. We can use personal statements that can sound like "I am choosing to let go of my resistance to change", "I am letting go of self-defeating", "I am allowing myself to change". Also emotionally focused technique can help to remove the resistance. After overcoming the resistance we should return to work with the beliefs. Find evidence with costs and benefits sheets and focus on development of new beliefs. We should keep it simple and work on one belief at a time.

My Journal

This practice has few steps. Please give yourself enough time and don't rush through it.

1. Copy the next chart and identify a few self-defeating beliefs you want to change. Fill the cells of the chart.

Belief	Emotions / Feelings	Behaviour

2. Choose one belief from the previous chart. Copy this chart to identify the costs and benefits. Don't base your judgement on morals but on its impact and how the belief affects your feelings, decisions, choices, relationships, joy and overall happiness. Costs and benefits can be illogical and irrational.

Belief:	
Costs	**Benefits**

Notes
Here you will write about your feelings, additional thoughts and problems caused by this belief

3. Based on previous practise create a new balanced belief.

   My new belief is:

   ...

   ...

   ...

4. Copy the new belief in a chart and complete it:

New belief:	
Costs	**Benefits**

Notes
Here you will write about your feelings, additional thoughts and problems caused by this belief

5. Memorize and repeat it frequently. Each time when you remember the old belief immediately replace it with the new one.

The next table shows some examples of old and new beliefs.

Old beliefs	New beliefs
People should like me because I am a nice person.	I am a nice person and some people don't have to like me. (People choose to like someone or not. It's individual's choice.)
If I am alone I must feel miserable.	I can be a good company to myself. (We can be alone and feel happy. Loneliness can be a problem and it needs attention.)
I should never feel angry.	Anger results from long-term frustration. Anger is bringing my attention to imbalance.
I should never be sad. I must be always be happy.	Be sad time to time is okay and normal. I don't have to be always happy. (Feelings point to something what might be out of balance and needs attention).

16. 3. When You Can't Change Beliefs

We may resist changing some beliefs about ourselves because they are enforced by emotional bias and past experience. When we are resistant we should identify their emotional attachments. Often resistance relates to past emotional hurts and rejections. Curiosity about the origin of self-beliefs would help. Once we understand how and why we preserve them we better know their functions. Consequently we reprocess emotions attached to these beliefs.

Let's Do It Now

1. In your journal write the belief you resist to change. Answer the group of questions to support and contradict your belief. Be open-minded and don't try to find logical reasons behind your belief.

Answers to Support :

How does my past support this belief (in my personal history, other people, friends, family, peers, teachers, and bosses)? What true is in my belief? What else could this belief mean? How does it fit or agree with my other beliefs? Is it the right time to change my belief? Is there something I learn from this belief? What and who can help me if I struggle with it? What would _ (somebody who I value) say about this belief? What does this belief say about me, my security, fear, denial, avoidance? What good I get from this belief? What can I do to alternate my thinking? What is the best thing that could happen when I maintain this belief? Is thinking this way helping me to feel good or to achieve my goals? Why is this belief important for me? Have I believed the same 1, 5, 10 years ago? If not what made me to create this belief? How will this matter in 1, 5, 10 years' time?

Answers to Reverse:
How does my past contradict to this belief (in my personal history, other people, friends, family, teachers, bosses)? Are my beliefs experience and factual or just my interpretations, emotional reasoning so this belief is one of them? Am I jumping to conclusions or is it my problematic patterns of thinking? What other explanations can argue that my belief is wrong? What are there other thoughts I could have instead of this belief? If I were being positive, how would my beliefs sound? If I was feeling good about my-self would be this belief valid? What would _ (somebody who I value or cares about me) say about this belief? What does this belief say about me, my security, fear, denial, avoidance? What bad do I get from this belief? What is wrong, emotional, irrational, negative or extreme in this belief? What is the worst thing that could happen when I maintain this belief? Is thinking this way helping me to feel good or to achieve my goals? Why do I want to change this belief? Have I believed the same 1, 5, 10 years ago? If not what made me to create this belief? How will this matter in 1, 5, 10 years' time?

2. Think about willingness to let go off this belief. Are you willing to let it go? Copy the following chart and fill it in.

My old belief:	
Evidence to support	Evidence to reverse
Am I willing to let go off this belief? Why not?	
My new belief: Reasons why I want to develop it:	

3. Write your new belief on an index card. Memorize it and practise as you did in Chapter 12.

THE STRONGEST YOU

17. MENTAL IMAGERY TO STRENGTHEN THE MIND

The mind and brain together can do a lot of good work. We can use the mind to regulate feelings and strengthen the pathways of good feelings that the brain creates in the body. Mental imagery is a technique using the brain and mind's ability to collaborate and positively respond to images.

17. 1. Let the Mind and Brain Work

Perhaps, we don't have sufficient understanding but we know that we can visualise, create mental images of objects, scenes, events or even ideas and feelings. Imagination comes from a neural network which spreads across a large area of the brain. This triggers neural associations. There is no substantial difference in what happens in the brain when we see something or when we imagine something. The brain responds similarly to both imaginative or physical. This is a quite an amazing capability of the brain. We can use this and intentionally create new neural connections. This is what we try to do when doing mental imagery.

Helpful Hints

We use imagination when we visualise something we have never seen, when remembering, thinking about past or future. Children use imagination in pretending games. We use imagination in creation, invention or resolving problems. The mind allows unlimited mental images. We can use this like in drama, performing arts, sports, athletic performance, leadership or marketing. Visualise and experience what you visualise.

In daily life we use mental imagery often in negative ways. We imagine something fearful, bad or tragic. With this we create emotions. If we can do it in negative ways there is no doubt we can do it in positive ways. We shouldn't waste these phenomenal capacities of the mind and the brain. We should be willing to experiment and use them for the best.

Let's Do It Now

To better understand, and perhaps overcome doubts about what has been said, we can experiment. We can trigger negative and positive feelings.

- Trigger negative feelings: Remember a situation that made you very unhappy and sad. Close your eyes and think profoundly about it. Imagine the details of that situation. Give it time. Visualise yourself in details, clothes you were wearing, how you were feeling, whole environment where it happened people, details of the place, colours, objects, smells, words and sounds, maybe even taste. Let the detail image create in the mind. Give it time. Try to employ your senses. Hold the mental picture about five to ten minutes. Observe reactions in your body and feelings.

- Trigger feeling good: Think about a situation that made you very happy and do the same as you did in the previous exercise.

- Trigger good feeling: Close your eyes and think about a person you profoundly like and love. Think about why and what you love about them, about good times you spend together, remember feelings when you are around them. Imagine their face; notice beautiful details you like, their smell, voice, touch or taste. Do it for five minutes and observe what it does to your feelings and body.

Compare your experiences and you might write about this experience in your journal.

17. 2. Powerful Mental Imagery

The mechanism of mental imagery remains a mystery; however, we know it relates to how the two sides of human brain think and process information. The left side of the brain thinks logically and processes sequentially. The right side thinks in pictures and processes simultaneously. Left side is more attuned to the outside world while the right side to the inner world and emotions. It seems that the right side of the brain "sees" the concerns related to us in bigger views.

When using guided mental imagery we experience psychological time, mental travelling. It happens similarly to when we are absorbed in activities such as creativity, solving problems and forget about the time and everything else. It's a normal state anybody can experience when daydreaming, planning, thinking about the past, other people and places. Guided mental imagery redirects focus and is far more than just the visual sense or mental activity. Although it has been called mental imagery it involves the whole body, emotions and senses.

Guided mental imagery is a gentle technique that directs imagination in proactive and positive ways. Because of the brain's adaptability involved guided mental imagery is specifically arranged, plus it becomes more effective over time. We use a variety of mental imagery depending on goals: alleviate stress, transform creativity, shift feelings about something, elevate good feelings, reduce negative feelings, promote balance and healing, etc. Mental imagery can be guided or self-guided.

17. 3. Try Self-Guided Mental Imagery

The following exercises are suitable for all, both advanced and beginners who respond well to visualisation and relaxation.

How to Do It

Before starting identify the target and desired feelings. Practice while sitting in a comfortable position in a quiet place and with closed eyes to deepen the experience. Assume a passive posture, breathe easily and hold the mental picture as long as it feels comfortable. Keep single focus and eliminate other thoughts.

- **Calmness:** Pick a word, phrase or prayer that makes you feel peace and calm. For example a phrase: I am feeling calm. Repeat the phrase few times aloud and memorize it. Think about how you feel when you are calm and relaxed. Close your eyes and visualize the phrase in the mind. Breathe and hold the mental picture in the mind. Mentally read the words or whisper to start. Hold onto the image of the word or phrase you chose. Practice until the desired feeling floods your body.
- **Specific relaxation**: Using autogenic instructions with mental images triggering sensory and muscle response: Close your eyes

and relax. Mentally scan and connect with the muscles that you are instructing. For example say, "Muscles on my face are relaxed", imagine the face is becoming relaxed. Let tension leave your face. Focus on feelings of relaxation spreading around your face, feel it. Add colours: relaxation is usually bright like sunshine or light, tension is usually dark. Let the dark leave your body and bright come in. Hold the image of a relaxed area for at least five minutes. This way you can address any problematic issue or location in your body. You can use this technique to decrease pain. Imagine pain as darkness residing in a painful area. Imagine that pain is leaving the problematic area to allow healing. Healing can be bright like sunrays. Let the dark leave your body and bright enter your body.

- **Let the negative emotions go**: Imagine negative emotion as dark heavy matter residing in your body, for example if you feel fear imagine a dark cloud in your head. If you feel sad you might feel tension and darkness around your heart. If you feel angry your stomach area might feel heavy and dark. Close your eyes to start imaging this darkness precisely placed in your body. Mentally instruct the darkness to leave. Visualize the darkness leaving your body. Give it time. Patiently move it further away and let it fly high into the sky where it disappears. Imagine positive emotion as light colour. Feel it entering your body to replace the negative emotion. Let the light push the residual darkness away. Allow the new emotion to develop. Hold the mental image at least for five minutes until you feel it.

- **Relax the whole body**: Follow the step as when addressing specific relaxation and continue the same way with other areas of the body. This practice takes longer as you move slowly through the whole body. Use autogenous instructions and gradually relax the muscles on your face, neck, shoulders, chest, back, arms, abdomen, legs, and feet. When you are done with relaxing the muscles imagine you are relaxed and light. Keep the image for few minutes until you feel it.

- **Let go of disturbing and negative thoughts**: Visualize negative thoughts as heaviness, darkness, the dark matter or the cluster of dark clouds. Keep it simple and specific. For example someone has recurring thought "She betrayed me" and feels sadness. They can visualize a negative thought and attached sadness all wrapped in black and residing on top of their chest. Gently imagine that the darkness is detaching from you, disturbing thoughts and feelings enveloped in darkness are leaving. Imagine your exhale pushes them away and far from you. Each breath blows them further, away until they float in the sky. Repeat until the darkness disappears. Imagine an empty space in your mind after the thoughts left and feel lightness. For about five minutes hold onto the feelings of lightness.

- **Create places to relax**: Imagine a soothing, calming place you have seen or visited; any imaginative or real places that give pleasant and joyful feelings. It can be picturesque nature with variety of pleasing shapes, shades, sounds or smells such as mountains, meadows, hills, valleys, lakes, seas, sky or horizons. Imagine the rich colours of the place, add the sounds and smells. For example you can imagine a sandy beach, turquoise sea, listening to the waves crushing, birds chirping, wind blowing. You might imagine waterfalls, water plopping, river floating, or other sounds that would go with your image. Close your eyes and after developing a specific relaxing image in the mind breathe easily while holding the image. Just breathe, keep the image and employ your senses. Do it until the relaxed feelings flood your body and you find comfort in them.

17. 4. Grow Stronger with Mental Imagery

Let's Do It Now

The following examples are scripts of mental imagery used to relax. You can experiment with them and create your own script to get what you might be looking for.

Self-guided Mental Imagery to Relax

Note: Read the script few times, record it and then follow the recording.

You can practice while sitting and start with the closed eyes. Bring awareness to your breathing, don't try to force it or control it. Just be… Imagine you are walking on a beautiful beach. You're barefoot and you feel the warm sand on your feet as you walk, as it touches the soles of your feet…Notice the details of your appearance and feelings in your body while walking on the beach… pleasantly warm and comforted. The beach is almost deserted as it expands across the horizon… …hear the hypnotic sound of the waves crashing on the shore…The sound is relaxing your body and mind… Look at the waves coming and going. See the sea's surface on the horizon. Look at the sky… At a distance see a sailboat as it slowly moves… Everything makes you very relaxed and you feel light, comforted, safe…As you walk, feel the sand on your bare feet, smell the fresh, salty scent of the sea… Breathe deeply… inhale…and exhale… feel more and more relaxed… See the birds in the sky flying gracefully in the wind…Feel the freedom of flying… and the air touching you…You are more and more relaxed… Feel the fresh breeze and the warmth of the sun on your face, your neck and shoulders are relaxed…Feel completely calm… Sit on the warm sand and feel it. Close your eyes, stretch your body and relax completely. Be comfortable and breathe the fresh air. Breathe deeply and enjoy the moment. Listen to the sound of the waves, coming and going. The rhythmic sound takes you into a deeper and deeper state of relaxation. Enjoy the peace and calmness. Breathe ……

Now, in a minute, you will come back to your place and this time… gradually start coming back… you're becoming more and more awake…slowly move your fingers, hands, toes and legs…gently move your arms and legs…make a gentle motion with your head …you are almost completely alert … open your eyes…you are alert and refreshed…

Guided Mental Imagery to Relax

Turn on the recording and follow instructions.

17. 5. Can You Project the Future?

This mental technique allows creating images in the relaxed state. It might feel like a dream but it can bring inspiration or messages. You should repeat the practice about five times or more within ten days for benefit. During practice you might experience the sequence of images or the same images appearing. What you do with them is up to your feelings or intuition and how you interpret them. Write notes at the end of each practice and review all notes after the set of mental imagery is finished. You can see this technique as self-exploration or try to understand the images based on how they match with personal life, emotional past or current needs. Be playful.

Description and Script: Project the Future

Before you start prepare your journal and pen to write about your experience. Practice in a private place, sitting with the closed eyes and focus on breathing. This practice can take a longer time and the rule is: Don't rush. Don't force anything, try to breathe naturally and be relaxed...

When you are fully relaxed observe any thoughts coming to mind but don't engage them, don't expand or force. Let the thoughts come and leave. Bring awareness to breathing. Give it time and let the breaths relax you…just breathe…there's nothing important only the breath….

Bring attention to personal future, one year from now. Imagine yourself in one year's time. Don't force and don't hang on anything. Just think about yourself a year from now. Let the shifting images come and go. Be a good observer. Notice their details. Look closely at them…What do you see? Where are you? What are you doing? Who are you with or are you alone? If you are in activity with others, who are they? Can you recognize those people? …Let the pictures grow in the mind … observe them... Just breathe and see the images….

Slowly move awareness to five years' time. Don't force any image, let them develop naturally. Think about yourself five years from now… Where are you? … It might be a place that you don't recognize or know... Observe the images as they develop. Don't get involved only notice details. What are you doing five years from now? Who are you with? Observe the pictures in the mind...don't force any understanding. See their details...the mental images have been creating... Spot the details... Just breathe and see them...

Move in time and now see the pictures of your life in ten years' time. Stay relaxed and focused. Breathe and observe as the images are created in your mind. Where are you... might be a place that you don't recognize or know... Observe the images as they develop. What are you doing ten years from now? Who are you with? Observe the pictures in the mind...don't force any understanding. See their details... Just breathe and see them... Notice their details as you are focused on a time of ten years from now. Let the images build in the mind... breathe... breathe and look at the images of your life ten years from now...

Slowly in the mind bring attention to your place and this time ... gradually you're becoming more and more aware ...make a gentle motion with your head ...you are almost completely alert ...Stay connected with your experience, open your eyes, take a pen and write your reaction to what you experienced. Write as much as you wish. Let your mind and heart lead your hand.

Repeat this practice as instructed.

17. 6. How to Enter Limitless Possibilities

This mental technique allows creating images in the relaxed state. Let the mind guide towards the hidden desires or wishes and it might feel like a dream. Repeat the practice about five times or more within ten days to benefit. Write notes at the end of each practice and review all notes after the set of mental imagery is finished.

Description and Script

Before starting prepare your journal and pen ready to record the experience. Practice in a private place, sitting with closed eyes and focus on breathing. This practice can take a longer time and the rule is No rush. Don't force the breath, try to breathe naturally and be relaxed.

When you are fully relaxed observe any thoughts coming to mind but don't engage them, don't expand or force. Let the thoughts come and leave. Bring awareness to breathing. Give it time and let the breaths relax you…just breathe…there's nothing important only the breath…. Give it a time and let the breaths relax you…just breathe…. bring the center of your awareness to yourself… your inner self…the most connected … the wisest of you…feel yourself… genuine you…your honest you…Allow yourself to enter the hidden.

Imagine that you're stepping into a field of limitless possibilities… you're surrounded by a field of limitless support…allow realizing of your greatest gifts and contributions…feel yourself as the center of your eternity… ask: what do I most deeply desire… what experience in my life is for me…what can I express through my life…what can I create in my life…how can I contribute to others and the world…your imagination allows entering all awareness of the mind...what is hidden within me? Let the mind bring you the answers…ask for them… notice the sensations you might feel…ask the deepest parts of yourself… breathe …breathe into your desires… as though you were inhaling the rich fragrance of truth and eternity. Fully welcoming and embracing them with each breath… ask: What is my next step...What am I able to experience…What am I able to express…What can I create…Can I contribute to my desires… Give it time. Wait for the answer from the deepest part of you….Breathe…

Sense when it's time and slowly in the mind bring attention to your room and this time …becoming more and more aware. Stay connected with your experience and open your eyes. Take a pen and write about your experience; anything you want, your reaction to it or describe images. Write as much as you wish. Let your mind and heart lead your hand.

Repeat this practice as instructed.

THE STRONGEST YOU

18. BECOME STRONGER THROUGH MINDFULNESS

Why should we learn mindfulness, relaxation or meditation? How do we benefit from them? How can we incorporate them in life?

People can be too sceptical about the power of mindfulness or meditations. Perhaps understanding the basics behind this can help to overcome the resistance. There are many benefits of mindfulness and meditation. They:

- gently train the mind, help to develop non-judgemental thinking, lead towards conscious decisions, allow seeing opportunities.
- softly control feelings, improve emotions, increase relaxation response and overall improve functioning.
- help to stay grounded in personal life and connected with oneself.
- increase whole awareness and healthier choices.

18. 1. Understand Mindfulness

The human brain is made up of billions of cells called neurons, passing information by firing signals and producing electric activities. It was detected that these electric activities, measured in Hertz (Hz), are cyclic and they create patterns called brainwave patterns. Medical professionals use sensitive equipment to measure them. They record electric activity of the brain by placing electrodes over areas of the scalp. It's called EEG. Recorded electric activities in the brain help us to understand not only the brain but also mental and overall health. These patterns change based on one's physical and mental activities. For instance during waking hours the brain produces high frequency brainwaves called gamma. During the state of deep sleep the brain produces lower frequency brainwaves called delta. There is a range of brainwaves between gamma and delta.

In relaxation and meditation we exercise a state as just before we get up in the morning or before sleep, alpha brainwaves. We can produce deep relaxation or light sleep, theta brainwaves. In these states the brain doesn't process much information while it stays receptive and absorbent. Thus in meditation and relaxation we gently control the brain's electric activities. Practically, we interrupt the electric cycle to produce the one we want. We allow the brain in a gentle way to relax and absorb. This can be hugely beneficial. Particularly in busy days when we tend to ruminate, we are overstimulated or restless, lack restorative sleep, experience unwelcome feelings or when the body is unwell.

Feeling Pleasure

The other important benefit from guided relaxation and meditation is the brain's production of natural good chemicals, endorphins, such as beta-endorphins or dopamine. These chemicals are associated with happy and relaxed feelings. They are beyond enlarged mental clarity when the right side of the brain (right hemisphere) creates images and allows experiencing pleasure. It's amazing that this effect can last hours or days. With the regular practice the adaptability of the brain allows changes; the brain changes by itself.

Helpful Hints

The patterns of brainwaves tell much about health. People suffering Attention Deficit Disorder (ADD) lack beta brainwaves. People suffering Anxiety Disorders have an abundance of beta waves. By changing mental and physical activities we can help to improve brain functioning. It's interesting to know that when we close our eyes the brain responds. We reduce stimulations and the brain changes the frequency of brainwaves.

Mindfulness, Meditation, Relaxation

Essentially mindfulness is a full awareness, total involvement in a present moment. In formal mindfulness we deepen connection with our inner experience, thoughts and emotions, how the body feels and physical sensations in the body. We don't assume any experience, don't force any mental activities. We try to observe what happens within us, take a note of thoughts. We don't try to direct or judge, rather to gently recognize. We can formally practise mindfulness as meditation or less formally we can exercise it within other activities. When practising mindfulness we don't engage in thinking, problem solving, analyzing or synthetizing. We rather use the right brain hemisphere which thinks in pictures. Mindfulness practise helps us to learn how to let the thoughts come and go, not hold on to them.

In this chapter we practise meditation and relaxation. Although they share similarities they slightly differ. Their effects on the body, mind and feelings are comparable. Both are skills that almost anyone can develop and improve with practising. In both we can experience states of the unfocused, floating or passive mind, frequently filled with shifting images. Formal relaxation can be passive or we can mentally rehearse relaxing commands, use autogenic phrases. In relaxation we deliberately focus to decrease stress and increase the relaxation response. Relaxation can have different forms such as progressive muscle relaxation, guided imagery or simple relaxing breathing. What do we know about meditation?

- The mind remains rather passive and still, we might pay attention to bodily sensations, non-judgemental self-awareness, passive attendance to the happenings in the mind, deliberate focus on some aspects (calmness, love, kindness or peace, for example), or use statements and autogenic phrases.

- Regular meditation over time increases self-awareness and connection with one's inner world.

- Regular practice can profoundly regulate mental habits, reduce distractive and ruminative thoughts.

- Advanced meditators can develop deeper insight into their experience or they might experience recurring mental images.

- Group meditators can report similar experience during synchronized meditations or some meditations can invoke state of tranquility or trance. Meditations can trigger intensive sensory experiences, visual, auditory or tactile or seizure like experience.

- Meditations can be passive or have goals.

- Meditation improves stress response, reduces distress and

increases positive feelings.

- The most important psychological benefits are that regular practice can positively impact the relationships with self, build concentration and develop mindfulness in daily life.

Despite advanced science we still don't fully understand the brain, mind and consciousness which play crucial roles in experiences during meditations. Some people create mysticism around meditations. Perhaps, because people are driven by meanings we try to interpret the abundant mental images experienced in meditations and create myths. Essentially, meditation can be seen as an internal, maybe intimate, experience and we have a free choice to interpret it.

18. 2. Learn Relaxation Techniques

The term relaxation has quite a wide use and it can include any activities that relax the mind and body. For some people it can be dancing, drawing, listening to the music, walking, socializing, etc.

Relaxation as a technique activates relaxation response in the body. We can see it as helping a body to reenergize, calm and improve feelings. Once we calm the mind and body we are open to being positive and balanced. Relaxation response is a reaction in the body, the opposite of stress response. We should include regular relaxation in our schedule regardless how busy it might be. At times just brief relaxing breathing can provide quick relaxation and it can be done almost anywhere.

We can relax in different positions. We can experience full physical ease while stretching the body lying flat on the back as shown in the picture. Some people might fall in sleep, doze and we should allow enough time to return gently; gradually attending the present moment. Progressive muscle relaxation or relaxing breathing are perform while sitting upright.

Relaxation Pose

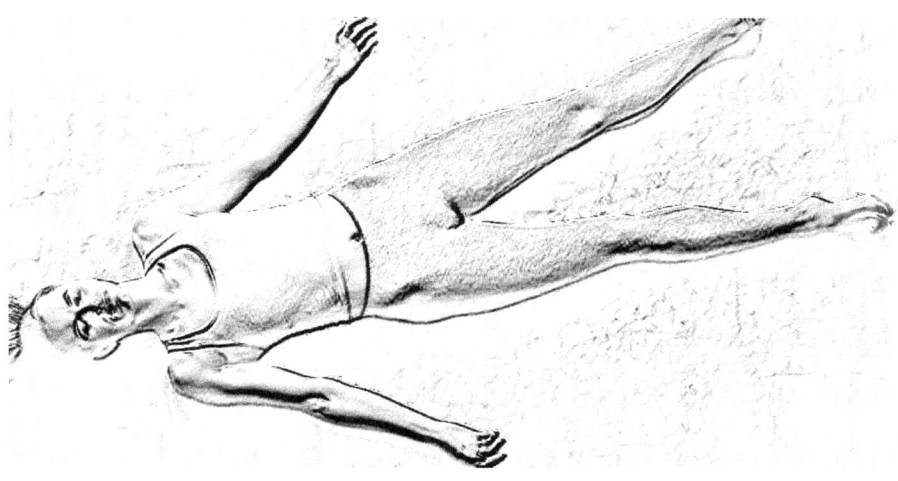

Relaxation with Autogenic Phrases

This practice can be done anytime, before going to sleep or in the middle of a day. It can be done as self-guided or we can use a recording and follow instructions.

Autogenic phrases

With every autogenic phrase we bring attention to the referred body part. Start from the top towards the soles of the feet.

Let's Do It Now

Self-guided Relaxation with Autogenic Phrases

Read the phrases underneath a few times and try to remember the phrases. After you are comfortable, close your eyes and try self-guided practise. In the mind instruct yourself by using the following phrases.

My mind is calm and silent

The top of my head feels soft and relaxed

My forehead is relaxed

My eyelids are heavy and eyes relaxed

My face is relaxed and smooth

My neck feels relaxed

My throat is relaxed

My chest feels relaxed and open

My shoulders are relaxed

My arms are heavy and relaxed

My hands are relaxed

My stomach feels light and relaxed

My legs are heavy and relaxed

My feet are relaxed

My whole body is relaxed

My body is relaxed and rejuvenated

My mind and body are completely relaxed

Guided Relaxation with Autogenic Phrases

Use the recordings included with this book. Assume the relaxation pose as in the picture. Turn the audio on, close your eyes and follow the script.

Notes: Don't be alarmed if you feel dozy after this practice. Take enough time before you get up. Fully move your body when you are completely aware and feel rejuvenated.

Progressive Muscle Relaxation

This popular technique is simple and it has been used over the century for its strong and immediate effects. Progressive muscle relaxation builds on the body-mind connection; mental tension can be reduced through the body. We contract and relax selected muscles to release stress "stored" in muscles as a consequence of emotional distress. People with injuries or chronic pain shouldn't practise and consult their doctors. We can practice daily and include progressive muscle relaxation in regular practice.

Let's Do It Now

Self-guided Progressive Muscle Relaxation

Review the following description and try to remember what to do. After you are confident, practise. While sitting in a chair with closed eyes and flat feet on the floor, contract the muscles for about seven seconds and let them relax for about the same time.

1. Breathe deeply, slowly exhaling after each breath. When you exhale imagine that the tension in your body is slowly beginning to disappear.

2. Close your hands into fists. Hold it for seven seconds…now let go of the fists and open your hands… Your hands feel heavy… Feel the tension disappears.

3. Tense your forearms as if you were showing off your muscles in both arms. Hold it….and release. Feel the tension disappears. Your arms feel heavy.

4. Tense your triceps extending your arms in front of your body. Hold… and release…Feel the tension decreases and disappears.

5. Tense the muscles in your forehead by raising your eyebrows as much as you can…Hold….and release…Picture your muscles are becoming soft and relaxed…

6. Tense the muscles around your eyes by squeezing them shut… Hold… and relax…Feel a sense of deep relaxation spreading out all

over that area...

7. Tense your jaw by opening your mouth very wide until you stretch those muscles...Hold...and release...Let your jaw drop... They feel heavy. The tension gradually disappears.

8. Tense the muscles in the back of your neck as if you were going to touch your back with your head. Focus only on tensing the muscles in your neck...Hold...and release...

9. Tense the muscles in your shoulders raising them as if you were going to touch your ears with them...Hold...and release... Feel the tension disappears.

10. Tense the muscles in your chest by inhaling deeply...Hold the breath...and exhale slowly...Imagine all the tension in your chest is slowly disappearing as you exhale...

11. Tense the muscles in your abdomen as if you were to touch your belly button to your backbone...Hold...and relax. Imagine a wave a relaxation spreading across your stomach.

12. Tense your muscles in the thighs as if you were showing the muscles...Hold...and release...Feel as your muscles are stretched and completely relaxed.

13. Tense the muscles in your feet slowly pointing your toes towards you...Hold ...and release. Your feet feel heavy. Feel the tension disappears.

14. Now you're going to do the opposite, pointing your toes in front of you...Hold...and release... Feel the tension disappears.

Stay calm and breathe normally. Imagine a wave of relaxation is slowly spreading throughout your body...starting at your head and gradually penetrating each group of muscles down your body until it reaches your feet...eliminating any residual tension. Finish the practice with few controlled breaths. Open the eyes and feel relaxed and rejuvenated.

Guided Progressive Muscle Relaxation

Use the recordings included with this book. Assume the relaxation pose as in the picture. Practise while sitting in a chair with closed eyes and flat feet on the floor. Turn the audio on, close your eyes and follow the script.

18. 3. Self-Fulfilment through Meditation

Learning to meditate requires patience. It is a gradual process to develop. Similarly as any other skills we start from their development and regularly through practice we strengthen them. Imagine that we are learning to read in a new language; firstly we learn the alphabet, the sounds of letters, then simple words and lastly read sentences before reading books and understand what we read. We have to take it easy and don't expect much at the begining. With persistence, open-mindedness and curiosity almost anybody can learn meditation. We exercise the non-judgemental mind while sitting for a few minutes and attending to the silence.

We should start with realistic goals: sit for a short time, five to six minutes, never set an alarm to finish and keep a clock in sight. To finish gently open the eyes, check the time and softly end. Meditation requires easiness about building time to tolerate quietness. The goal is sitting quietly until we find comfort in it. Regular practise and daily commitment makes it easier. The silence becomes more comfortable. When we relax easily only then we can build time. People respond differently and we must wisely choose the length of time. Regularity is crucial and we shouldn't give up. The indicator that we are ready to stretch time is focus and joy. Effortless, non-judgemental sitting, letting thoughts come and go, enjoying the stillness and silence are the signs that we are ready to experiment.

Some people might be discouraged, can't sit in quietness, can't stop thinking or they are not patient. If this happens we should try to understand the reasons. The silence can be disturbing when people are anxious, depressed, ruminative, chronically stressed. The silent meditation is not good for them. They should learn relaxation techniques, use guided mental imagery or other guided techniques. Once they learn to relax they can experiment with silent meditation, with music in the background or guided meditation.

Every practice should be done while sitting and with closed eyes to eliminate stimulation. Silence increases awareness of a current moment. We can pay attention to breathing and gradually stop noticing the breath. Some people prefer dim light, closed curtains or burning candles to deepen their experience. We should avoid practising when we are too tired, after heavy meals or after drinking alcohol. The most effective time is early morning meditation when nature and people are waking up. Meditation can't be rushed so we must allow enough time. Often the body and mind signal when to end.

Silent Meditation

Let's Do It Now

Designate a quiet place that provides you comfort and privacy, and where you can engage a regular practice. Remove all distractions. Ideally be alone in the room or with other meditating or relaxing people. Maintain fresh air and comfortable sitting. Bring a clock to where you can see it. Sit on the floor in the yoga easy sitting pose with crossed legs, straight spine, hands rested on the thighs and palms facing up. Another option is straight but comfortable sitting on a chair with feet flat on the floor, hands rested on the thighs and back relaxed and straight. Gently roll the shoulders back to open the chest, lightly close the eyes and focus on breathing. Decide for how long you will sit. Check the time and close your eyes. Focus on breathing. Take a few relaxing breaths and "tune in" by bringing attention inwardly. Try to pay attention to breathing and what happens in the body. If you have undesired thoughts notice them and don't engage them. Let them come and go. Repeat it many times, over and over. Try to maintain the calm mind. To finish gently open the eyes and look at the time. If you didn't meet your goals don't judge it. Gently close your eyes again and attend to your breath. Repeat this daily until you're ready to stretch the time.

Note: Sometimes it is useful to take written notes about experiences, describe what happened and record the progress. Some people are very responsive and can move faster to meditations with no time limit.

Others need a slower pace and steady practice at first. Try to be sensible and respond to your feelings to find comfort and your way. Don't force if you can't progress.

Our ultimate goal is to sit in the quietness with no concerns about time, with the passive, unfocused, floating mind and shifting mental images. Once we enjoy, it becomes available anytime and anywhere.

Saying Words in Focused Meditation

Focused meditation follows all the general principles as mentioned before but it has a different goal: we echo the words as a broken record repeats the same lyrics. Repetition might appear strange but it's powerful and has positive impact on feelings. We should learn focused meditation to improve our mental and emotional state.

Let's Do It Now

You can experiment with different words and decide which could work the best. Try the sentence "I accept myself". Close your eyes and repeat it slowly, softly, with full attention and focus. Whisper it for three minutes. To finish open the eyes and then observe the effects it has on you.

Description

Choose a word, words or statements of your focus to generate desired feelings. Write them down, play with the words until you are certain about them. Then memorize the words. In meditation gently say them over and over.

Linguistically and by meanings some words are more powerful than others and we can choose them by the goodness they represent. We can use them alone, such as forgiveness, love, peace, acceptance, happiness, blessings, courage, health, balance, gratefulness, appreciation, joy, self-acceptance, compassion. There is no prescribed time for doing this and five to seven minutes is reasonable. Practice the same focused meditation daily for twenty one or more days if you wish to deepen your experience.

Let's Do It Now

Choose a word, words or statement. Decide how long you will practise. Start as silent meditation. After few relaxing breaths whisper the chosen words; literally be as a broken record and focus only on the sound of your voice and the meaning of the words. To finish open the eyes. Once you meet the goal sit in silence for about a minute with closed eyes.

Note: Focused meditation can have a variety of goals such as personal wellbeing, global concerns or concerns of loved ones.

Examples of words for focused meditation:

Forgiveness: I forgive myself, I forgive to all involved, I feel free of blame, I am free of guilt

Anger: I am letting go of my anger, I am in peace, I am calm

Hurt: I am letting go of past hurts, I am free of hurts, I feel happy and loved

Self-esteem: I love myself, I am letting go of my old beliefs, I feel blessed and loved, I feel good about myself, I am who I am

Acceptance: I accept myself, I accept my life, I accept my past, I accept my flaws, I accept the flaws of others, I accept limits, The world is full of contrast and I accept it, I am alright with my imperfection

Sadness: I am letting go of sadness, I am feeling balanced, I am choosing to let go of sadness, I feel worthy of feeling good

Fear: I am letting go of fear, I feel secure, I choose courage, I feel strong, I am brave to face difficulties, I am choosing security

Trust: I trust to myself, I trust everything that comes in my life, I am confident I can handle difficulties, I can cope with challenges, I trust the better time is on its way, I do my best all the time, I trust that everyone does the best, There is good for everyone and for me

Peace and love: Peace and love to everyone, Peace and love in me and around me, I feel loved, Love is for everyone, Love is free, Peace and blessing to us.

THE STRONGEST YOU

19. NON-JUDGEMENTAL THINKING CAN HELP

Sometimes judgemental thinking is not beneficial and we should learn non-judgemental thinking. Being non-judgemental is not easy. It's almost opposite to what we are expected to do. From childhood on we are encouraged to be judgemental, have and express ideas and opinions. Judgements in life can turn unconstructive. Self-judgements can be too harsh or misleading. We might be too quick, meaninglessly preserve judgements that don't do good to anyone. Judgemental thinking can develop into dysfunctional thinking patterns and judgements become dysfunctional. We might even not be aware of them. Sometimes it is better to be neutral. We should let get go of judgements and practise open-mind thinking.

Non-judgemental thinking doesn't mean to see a silver lining where it isn't, nor is it false positivism. The goal of non-judgemental thinking is to break the bonds we develop with judgements. Not everything is black and white, good or bad, right or wrong and we should be able to non-judgementally acknowledge it. Non-judgemental thinking also helps to stay unbiased and without emotional involvement. It can bring new insight, open the view. It can improve how we relate to an issue, other people or ourselves. It decreases stress response and makes us less concerned. Sometimes we rush to judge and judgements grow into beliefs we hold onto them. We might forget they are just thoughts that we resist changing. Just because we are too judgemental we may refuse to accept reality, facts or truth. Sometimes we might be trapped in negativity just because we can't let go of judgements. We might dwell on our rightness and wrongness of others; resist adapting when necessary or draining relationships by judgements.

19. 1. Letting Go of Judgements

The following technique intentionally uses non-judgemental thinking and teaches how to cultivate this. We can apply it in situations or issues related to relationships, judgements about ourselves, other people, etc. We should practise it often to gradually develop a less judgemental attitude. Also we should cultivate it to reframe dysfunctional thinking patterns such as black and white thinking, emotional filtering and reasoning, dwelling or ruminating which relate to judgemental thinking.

Let's Do It Now

1. Identify and write a judgement you want to change.

2. Describe and write the reasons for letting go of it. Accept the reasons.

3. Replace the judgements with facts.

4. Create a non-judgemental statement that can replace your judgement. Write and read it. Practise its acceptance. Try to think in terms "It is as it is". Don't judge your judging.

5. Describe changes you notice in acceptance, emotions and feelings as you practice non-judgemental stance.

This technique works well with the following issues: improve self-esteem, develop more assertive communication, improve relationships, reduce fear, decrease sadness, reduce stress, control self-defeating and negative beliefs.

20. INTO AUTOMATIC THOUGHTS

The automatic negative thoughts can be like monsters; sneaky, malicious and often we are not aware of them. When we increase self-awareness we recognize how they inhibit good feelings and influence choices and behaviour. Rational thinking can be suppressed by automatic thoughts. The automatic thoughts seem to appear by surprise and abruptly. In this practise we try to catch automatic thoughts negatively influencing self-esteem.

How To Do It

This technique requires some preparation. Read points 1 – 3 thoroughly. Then read them again and record yourself.

1. Close your eyes and take few relaxed breaths and start focusing on what you want to get from this exercise: you want to know hidden negative beliefs. Use your breath to relax and give enough time to achieve calmness. Do not rush through, don't be judgemental and try to notice thoughts as they come through. Once fully relaxed mentally invite your inner critic but stay non-judgemental and self-observant. Use the following questions to navigate your insight. Listen to the recording: "Can you hear the words of self-criticism? Give it time. What does the inner critic sound like? Is it a voice of someone you recognize? What does it say? What words can you hear? Notice the critic's words. Does it say what you should or shouldn't, you must or mustn't, is it disapproving your actions, thoughts or feelings? Don't fight it just observe and attend your mind. Let the negativity talk. Don't judge it. As the negativity is getting stronger pay attention to feelings. What do you feel? Let the feeling grow; feel, observe and be watchful…." Pause and attend to your mind for as long as you might need.

2. In the relaxed mind you should be receiving shifting images. Stay connected with your feelings, and without distractions start writing. Let your mind to lead your hand and write about your experience. Don't try to understand or be logical; let the mind lead and decide to finish. If you think too much about what to

write or you can't recall thoughts or images, stop writing. Put the pen and notepad away while staying calm and continue to the next.

3. Turn on the recording: "Close your eyes, focus on breathing and attend to the quietness. Give it time. Slowly direct attention to what you want to get out of this exercise: feel positive, nurtured and be open to kindness and support. Do not rush and attend to the thoughts that come through and breathe. In the calm mind play with the words love, acceptance, kindness, support. Let the mind create images of them: they might be the words, sounds. Repeat after me. I'm love. I'm acceptance. I'm kindness. I'm support. Just breathe, don't force the mind and try to be non-judgemental. Notice images in the mind….At this moment mentally repeat: I am okay… I trust…I feel good about who I am… My life is okay as it is. I desire to feel good and be happy. I am feeling good… Focus on breathing and slowly became aware of the time and place where you are. When you are ready open your eyes." Turn off the recording. Write about your experience but you don't have to force it.

Let's Do It Now

It takes approximately twenty-five minutes. Prepare your recording, journal and pen to take notes. Practice in silence. Turn the recording on and practise.

When you finish, review the notes. You should be able to identify automatic thoughts and perhaps emotional attachments to them. To change continue in the same manner as changing beliefs.

Note: You can repeat this practise a few times in two weeks to obtain more profound information and then review all your notes. You should be able to identify patterns, negative and dysfunctional automatic thoughts brought up by this practice. Be specific and write them down. Your next target should be to change them the same way as you would change beliefs.

21. DON'T FIXATE ON NEGATIVE

Have you ever thought about people who put effort, skills and energy to create our comfortable life? How many people had to and have to work hard to make our daily life easy? We might take it for granted but there are still many people not having the comfort we consider standard. Think about traveling, electricity, technologies, food, cosmetics, restaurants, schools, medicine, you name it. There are many things we daily use or do and we forget to appreciate. We fail to realize not all people are as fortunate as we are.

When we shift our fixation on what we miss and acknowledge what we have, we automatically elevate our feelings.

We shouldn't forget to appreciate and value only when we lose. Gratefulness and appreciation are uplifting feelings with elevating vibration. We don't deny missing something but by seeing values in daily life we boost real positivity. When we focus on what is available rather on what we miss. Gratitude creates positive feelings, optimism, and promotes awareness. It strengthens the resistance to negativity. When we appreciate we stop fixiating on the negative and move towards the positive; to that we have, possess, use, do or what is given to us.

Along with appreciation we want to develop the habit of forgiving. In life not every story has a happy ending and forgiveness is a strong therapeutic release. Forgiveness is actually fairly self-concerned. We forgive mostly to help ourselves, not so much to help wrong doers. Forgiveness is the way to learn lessons and move on. We might be stuck in the turmoil of negative emotions like jealousy, blame, disapproval, self-pity, disappointment, etc. when holding bitterness. Sometimes people resist forgiving because they fear that by doing so they approve the wrong, become vulnerable or weaker. As the matter of fact, the opposite is the truth.

We forgive to become stronger, wiser and leave the bad behind. Even if we forgive we still should deal with consequences of wrong doing. Forgiveness triggers good feelings and completely changes emotional charge around an issue or wrong doers. It contributes to healing from the damage done. This healing doesn't have to be conditional upon the offenders' punishment. By forgiving ourselves and others we alleviate negative feelings that burden us.

Both, gratitude and forgiveness have the power to take us out of negativity. Make a space for new, elevated feelings.

21. 1. Gratitude Techniques

To create a powerful gratitude list we don't search for big things rather validate less noticed things that have a positive impact. We try to recognise aspects of us, others, work, nature, labour of other people and professionals, etc. We can be more appreciative, generous and spiritual. Focus on human qualities, peace, freedom, and so on. There are limitless reasons to be grateful.

Let's Do It Now

1. Write a list of ten ordinary things about people, actions or services. For example "My mom picks up my daughter from school", "Mobile telephone", "Electricity in the house"

2. For each item ask and answer: "What would be different in my life without this (name the thing)? What would I miss if I didn't have this (name the thing)?"

3. Review the list and express thankfulness for every item on your list. Focus on good feelings.

Note: Create a new gratitude list or use the one you have. Over the next five days review and change five items on the list daily. For new items repeat the step 2 and 3.

The more often we notice positive aspects of life, the faster appreciative feelings develop. We should try to incorporate gratefulness and appreciation into daily life. Often we should create written gratitude lists and modify them; have them accessible as a reminder that in many ways we are blessed.

Gratitude and Self-esteem

Commitment to gratitude and appreciation can be used for almost anything including us to improve self-esteem. Often we forget to appreciate ourselves, our qualities, skills, abilities, achievements. We can develop a gratitude list. Write ten positive items, good actions, personal traits or possessions. Modify the list, have it visible and remind yourself that you are grateful for the items on the list. Always we should check feelings when working with gratitude lists.

21. 2. Forgiveness Techniques

It might be challenging at first to forgive and the following techniques can be practised often until feelings improve. People can experience emotional and vibrational shift when they intentionally forgive. The best start is to sit in a quiet place with closed eyes, taking a few relaxing breaths and relax. Only then gradually bring attention to forgiveness and apply technique #1 or #2. These techniques take about fifteen minutes including relaxation.

Let's Do It Now

Forgiveness Technique # 1

Read the following paragraph and then practise.

Before you start decide what you want to forgive: review the issue or doing wrong that you forgive, include people who you want to forgive to, decide how you want to think and feel about the issue and people involved after you forgive. Then relax and gradually bring attention to the issue. In the mind play with the image of being free from the negativity you hold until you forgive, and benefits forgiveness can bring. Create an intention that forgiveness can stay with you, focus on trust that you can forgive and remove resistance. Mentally say: I allow forgiving. I don't resist forgiveness. I want and I can change my thinking and feelings around this issue". Choose your own words, don't rush and give enough time to the mind to play with the image of forgiving. Observe your feelings and be non-judgemental. Be patient and kind to yourself. Mentally start saying, "I am choosing to forgive__ (selected issue). I want to forgive to feel free from __ (negative feelings and thoughts). I am forgiving to _ (selected issues)". Mentally repeat these statements for about five minutes.

To finish say aloud, "I live in the now and I forgive (issue)" or create your own statement. Take few breaths, open your eyes and write the forgiveness statement on an index card or a sticky note and carry it with you as a reminder.

Let's Do It Now

Forgiveness technique #2

This technique is beneficial when you have unresolved issues with someone and you can't let go of hurt. Read the following paragraphs and then practise.

Before you start decide what you want to forgive: review the issue or wrong doing that you forgive, include people who you want to forgive, decide how you want to think and feel about the issue and people involved.

In the relaxed mind imagine that you can access an eternal source (energy, psyché, soul, spirit, goodness, God, purity, the Sun, the Universe.) Imagine that this source is with you and ask it to assist your forgiveness. Imagine that this source is a shining light and you can merge into it and become that light. Let the image in your mind grow and mentally say, "I am an unlimited source. I can forgive". Think of people involved in the issue and you want to forgive. In the mind visualize shining pillars of light, one is yours and the other one is the other party. Imagine them as the same source as yours. Be kind, patient and give it time.

Mentally express your feelings and intention to forgive. Ask the sources to help and accept your forgiveness. Mentally say, "I forgive myself and _ (people). We did the best that we could at the given time. I live in the now. I forgive". Picture the pillars and lights connect. Observe feelings and hold the image of forgiveness.

To finish take few breaths, open your eyes and write forgiveness statements on an index card or a sticky note and carry it with you as a reminder.

Note: Both techniques might need repetition to become familiar with them; then their benefits grow. You might write about your experiences in your journal.

THE STRONGEST YOU

22. PRACTISING EMOTIONAL FOCUS

Focus on emotional reprocessing is therapeutic and healthy. Essentially, we don't need anybody to reprocess painful emotions, even if issues relate to other people. Emotions are internal experiences that can change without others. The technique described in this chapter might seem obscure or too complicated. Someone might be resistant to try, while others like its peculiarity. Once we learn and experience its power we can become more enthusiastic and use this technique in its simplistic way. Overall this technique can have powerful results, regardless of whether we like or dislike it. In here we tap specific points with two or three fingers while thinking and talking about a selected issue. We genuinely vocalize feelings and sincere thoughts. Idea of tapping originates in acupressure and kinesiology. It's believed that negative emotions block energy and once we enter kinetic energy onto specific meridians (flows of energy) it removes the existing blocks.

There are many reasons why this technique works. Although it may be overlooked, the power of this technique resides in a combination of prolonged single focus, saying the truth, being honest, genuinely express feelings and thoughts. We use self-suggestions and incorporate new ways of thinking, thus alternating feelings.

We thrive when we can honestly self-express. We want to openly express feelings without fearing of judgement. We want to voice what we genuinely think but many times we can't do it. Often we have to suppress or mask, and that's why emotional focus is helpful. It allows free venting and restructuring negative thoughts. We can reprocess feelings without the fear that someone would be hurt.

The beauty is that we don't to talk to people who are behind our suffering which makes this technique comfortable and safe. The rule is: say aloud the bottled-up feelings, unwanted thoughts, and openly express without anyone around. Once we learn this technique its practise becomes quite easy. Most important is honesty and truthfulness. This technique takes approximately ten minutes and with practice we will be able to use it in just a few minutes.

Gently Tap Selected Points:

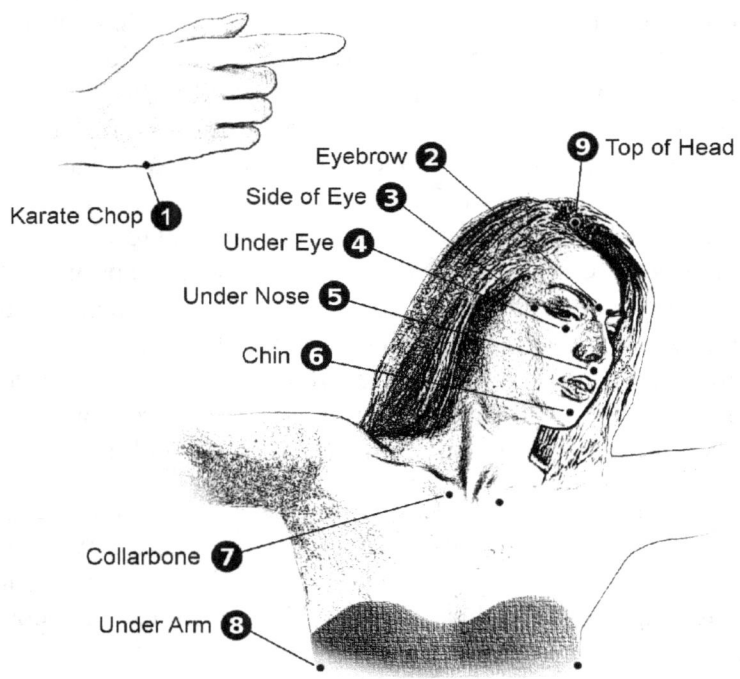

22. 1. Technique to Reprocess Emotions

With this technique we can focus on emotional reprocessing of a number of issues. Especially this technique can work wonders when people hold or overly control their thoughts and feelings.

This technique can be used in two ways:

1. One time for an immediate release from undesired emotions or conflicts. Problems can be related to anger, jealousy, fear, courage, blame, guilt, criticism, negativity, insecurity, loss, sadness, etc.

2. The other way of using is when we try to resolve profound issues such as beliefs, negative attitude, grieving, self-esteem, acceptance, past hurts, challenging relationships, weight man-

agement, pain, traumatic experience, communication, etc. We address the same issue and repeat this technique daily until we feel change.

Note: We choose an issue at first and then formulate statements while practising.

Let's Do It Now

Review the picture with tapping points. Use your fingers and locate the points on your body to become aware of them: Start at the top of your head and move downward; karate chop is side of any hand. Gently tap two – three times each point using point, middle and ring fingers. Use both hands at the same time; left hand taps left side and right hand taps right side. Once tapping through all points start at top of head and repeat it in the same manner. There is no rigid number of tapping. When you are confident with the points try the next example to learn this technique.

Note: In the future when using this technique you should be playful and honest. It will become easier with practice. Be creative and try your way of doing it.

Illustration: Reprocess Fear

Note: If you feel fear you can try this to tackle it. Learn this technique, rehearse at first and then do it again with high awareness of a problem. Modify statements as you might wish.

Targeted Issue: Fear

Desired outcome: Let go of fear

Sequence #1

Note: Genuinely accept yourself and an existing issue. Be aware of how you feel.

Say aloud while tapping only karate point, "Even though I feel fear I genuinely like and accept myself". You can say something similar like

"Even though I feel fearful, I genuinely like myself", "Even though I feel insecure and vulnerable I accept all these feelings", "Even though fear runs my life, I like myself", "Even though I am holding fear in my body, I like myself".

Sequence #2

Note: Honestly express thoughts and feelings. Recognize people if they are part of the issue and acknowledge negative impacts in your life.

Say aloud while tapping with both hands. After each statement tap next tapping points. Tap the top of your head and say, "These feelings make me poorly", tap eyebrows, "Fear makes my life difficult", tap side of eyes, "This fear develops conflicts", tap under eyes, "I feel it in every cell of my body", tap under nose, "My fear is shameful", tap chin "I hate feeling fearful", tap collarbone, "I am angry because I can't control my fear", tap under arms, "This fear blocks my mind and my actions", tap top of your head "I am ashamed of my fear", tap eyebrows, "I am fearful", tap side of eyes, "I feel foolish when I am afraid", tap under eyes, "It's not fair I have to deal with it", under nose "I hate this fear", collarbone, "I feel trapped in fear", under arms "It's debilitating", top of head" Why I can't let go of fear?"

Sequence # 3

Note: Express desired outcome, your choices & changes. In this example you want to feel free of fear. Name desired feelings.

Say aloud while tapping top of head, "I am choosing to be free of fear", eyebrows, "I don't need fear", side of eyes, "I am choosing to let it go of my body", under eyes, "I am giving permission to my body to release the fear", under nose, "I am letting go of the fear", chin, "I don't need to hold fear and I am choosing to let it go now", collarbone, "I am choosing to release fear from my mind and body", under arms, "I am allowing myself to be free of fear", top of head, "I am choosing to be free of fear", eyebrows, "I am brave to face the difficulties", side of eyes, "I am allowing myself to be courageous", under eyes, "I can be free of fear", under nose, "Fear has to go", chin, " I'm letting go of fear".

Sequence #4

Note: Express that everything you have done works, be bold and say you are free of an issue. Here you tap only one point, karate chop or top of your head.

Say aloud, "I trust that this works", "I feel free, "I am free of fear", "I feel relaxed", "I am confident", "I let go of fear", "I trust to myself", "I'm relaxed and free of fear", "I am grateful to my mind and body for letting go of fear", "I am grateful for new emotions filling my body", "I feel happy and free of the fear".

Finish with relaxing breathing: deep inhale through nose and full exhale through mouth. Repeat it few times.

Note: You might need to repeat the whole exercise one more time.

What's next?

Generally, start with closed eyes and "tune-in" by taking few controlled breaths. Then start gently tapping while expressing feelings and thoughts. You might prefer closed eyes to deepen the focus and experience.

22. 2. Let's Start

1. Choose a target (issue, problem, feeling) and desired outcome.

You can write it, define what you want to get from this, whether to release a "hot" feeling or resolve a deeper issue.

Example how to choose a target:

Thoughts: "The fear I feel is debilitating. I am afraid of the meeting with my boss tomorrow. He might be angry with my last decision. I am afraid I won't be able to express why I have done it. I know it was the best choice and I couldn't have done anything else."

Chosen target: Fear

Desired outcome: Confident self-expression

2. Express self-acceptance.

3. Express thoughts and feelings.

It is vital to feel okay with ourselves regardless the issues or struggles. The words of statements should come naturally from genuine self-expression but stick to the target and focus.

4. Express trust and positive attitude. Believe that changes can happen.

Let's Do It Now

Try your way of doing it:

1. Practise tapping points until you are confident with them.

2. Choose target.

3. Choose outcome.

4. Express and feel self-acceptance while tapping karate chop.

5. Express feelings, thoughts and negative consequences of an issue while tapping points as illustrated.

6. Express positive beliefs that changes in thinking and feeling can happen while tapping top of your head or karate chop.

7. Finish with relaxing breathing.

8. Take a note about shift in your feelings.

Note: Make sure you keep single focus and keep it simple. It's not important how many times you repeat tapping. Practise until you notice a change of feelings.

23. LAST HELPFUL HINTS

Here you find advice when downfalls and challenging experiences hit your life. Strategies include advised approach and attitude to improve. They direct your work and focus while you can use techniques from this book.

1. You experienced rejections, disappointments, betrayals, failures or you made mistakes.

Strategy: Focus on aspects surrounding that experience and identify the points you can improve, change or correct. Acknowledge what can't be changed, limits and uncontrollable. Try to figure out a way around it. Apply acceptance by recognizing it is as it is. The past has already happened and it can't be changed. Choose a different approach for the future. What will you do differently in future? Remind yourself of all sides not only the difficulties. Use it as a resource for learning and moving on. Use techniques from this book to develop acceptance, forgiveness and let go. Acknowledge how you feel and work on its improvement. Practise compassion and mindfulness.

2. You experienced a situation that attacked good feelings about yourself and hurt your self-esteem: anything that damaged self-esteem, decreased self-confidence or worthiness.

Remember that self-esteem acts as an emotional "immune system" and become accountable for good feelings about yourself. Healthy self-esteem can buffer other negative emotions. You should work on greater emotional resilience by maintaining healthy self-esteem. You should develop a habit to monitor and preserve healthy self-esteem.

Strategy: You must regularly let go of whatever negativity is residing in you. Monitor feelings about yourself and cultivate compassion. Be aware of the negative default of the mind and work on its control. Catch negative self-talks and criticism. With awareness you should correct dysfunctional thoughts, boost good feelings immediately as you notice negativity. Avoid being overly critical and rationally sum up facts. Focus on strengths and problem resolving. Use cognitive and behavioural techniques to develop new habits. Practise mindfulness and self-compassion.

3. Self-induced negativity, negative mindset, non-constructive and dysfunctional thinking.

It is natural to think about distress but you don't want to dwell or unconstructively think. Remember you can control the mind and not let it be wild. Distinguish when negative thinking comes from a problem you encounter or you allow the mind's default running.

Strategy: Reduce unnecessary thoughts and avoid dwelling, ruminating, analysing or fixating on distressing events. It is the matter of your focus and attention; focus on how to improve and change. Sometime life is too harsh or difficult. Not denying but resolving is critical in any situation. Occupy the mind by thinking how to advance not by pondering on problems. Use cognitive and behavioural techniques to move on. Improve the negative mind and restructure beliefs. Return to chapters to reprogramme beliefs and automatic mind. Practise mindfulness.

4. Overall negativity and seeing only the dark aspects.

The negative attitude never helps and you should remind yourself of problematic ways of thinking. Developing new habits is never easy and it doesn't happen without effort. You must try, learn to accept. Look at problems in bigger views. Remember that every cloud has a silver lining. There's always some learning in mistakes or difficulties and you can grow stronger.

Strategy: Redirect the mind from problems to resolution. You shouldn't fixate on problems by themselves. Build curiosity as new mental habits. It helps to recognize that if you don't how a problem should be resolved you might need to wait. Practise putting things in a bigger perspective. Ask questions related to solutions to gain insight. Sometimes there's not much you can do; you just need to accept and move on. Frequently stress builds up negativity and relaxation can return clarity and ease. Use mindfulness, relaxation, cognitive, behavioural and emotions focused techniques.

5. **Unresolved guilt and blame.**

These can be big and prevent you seeing beyond them. Guilty feelings are necessary in small doses. They provide feedback when someone does wrong. Guilt should motivate to correction and improvement. Not to become burdens that drags you down. Blame induces additional negativity and it doesn't help to advance. If guilt and blame stay as mindsets they can sabotage all attempts to feel happier.

Strategy: Address unresolved guilty feelings and blame. Acknowledge doing wrong, yours or someone else's actions. The best antidotes are kindness, compassion, gentleness. Try to receive or give forgiveness, directly or do it in the mind and emotionally reprocess. Sometimes guilt is self-generated and people may resist letting go of guilt. One might believe that living in guilt is necessary or it is a justifiable sort of punishment people deserve. The mind can allow forgiving and it shouldn't be seen as denial of responsibility. Take a lesson for the future. Change how you think about doing wrong. Letting go of blame and guilt can shift overall feelings. Then decide for strategies to improve. Practice forgiveness, cognitive techniques, mindfulness and emotionally focused techniques.

6. **Experiencing losses.**

Smaller or bigger losses are reality of life. Rarely do they arrive upon requests and always they bring unexpected turns. Depending on their impact recovering from losses can take a while. Especially losses of significant relationships are painful. It can take time to make peace with the loss and move on. After losses you can experience phases of grieving. Sometimes it's better to stop trying to understand why someone left you, betrayed or treated you as they did. Human behaviour can be peculiar and you don't always need to understand others. The most vital is to understand you. Use self-knowledge to your best benefit. You should put energy into learning how to live after a loss. You need kindness and positive emotions, allow them. You must trust that time helps but you must help yourself. Sometimes you might need to convince yourself that you can't afford to give up. You need hopes and change; allow life without whatever a loss took away. If you struggle to keep hope you might turn attention to whomever and whatever is left. Reasons that you have to accept and go on might be your children, parents, friends or important values that you cherish.

Strategy: Focus on building strong positive beliefs. Allow sad feelings and grieve if you need it. Accept your legitimate feelings and don't try to suppress them. Distress becomes less severe with passing time. Emotions fade and feelings change. Avoid analysing and trust that later, when you'll be emotionally better, you can understand more. Try to put losses in a big picture. Think in timeline and life as a whole. Acknowledge aspects of life that a loss has impacted. Recognize both, good and bad sides. Consider exploring new activities, reconnect or meet new people, address needs and wants created by the loss. Time after losses is not the best time to make significant decisions and don't rush. If you struggle after losses find a counsellor, support group and like-minded people. You should consider behavioural changes, try new things. You should be physically active to help the body fight the stress response. Jogging, running, cycling, kick-boxing or you might prefer hot yoga, karate, Taekwondo or other activities employing the mind and body. You should work on emotional reprocessing, practise relaxation, acceptance, mindfulness and letting go.

What's next?

Bring this book to a close. Continue practising to complete the 12 weeks. Carefully review your notes to identify the aspects you want to improve. Don't stop now.

Remember, "***In the mind and self, be The Strongest You.***"

ABOUT THE AUTHOR

"Perhaps, thanks to my own circumstances I redirect attention from what we can't do to what we can do. Put attention to the right place. Simply know ourselves and from there move towards improvement," says Szakal. "When my life lost momentum, when unprepared I was exposed to traumatizing stress, the approach I share through this book became a life saver. It helped me to come to terms with difficult challenges, carry on with life and continue to help others. The Strongest You is not a statement; it's the constructively used inner force. Any person can do it. The Strongest You is the catalyst for positive change through the powerful mind."

Now residing in Yorkshire, England Ivana Straska Szakal, M. A., a successful educator and mental health professional, brings inspiration and her unique style to help others. Writing her book with guided practice was inspired by her clients and personal challenges. Her vast experience encouraged her to develop a unique approach that any person can adopt.

Szakal's book introduces coaching of the mind towards positive transformation. The book explains how the automatic mode of the mind can cause a dysfunctional service. Following the lessons in these pages Szakal teaches how to reverse this. The reader is carried forward while purposefully using her approach tailored to individual's circumstances. Powerful techniques are learned, such as visualization, restructuring of thinking, emotional reprocessing, mindfulness, relaxation and more. The reader resets their minds in less than 12 weeks to move forwards on the path towards joyfulness.

Born in the former Czechoslovakia Szakal obtained her degrees and first work experience in management of educational projects in Bratislava, Slovakia. With two children and husband she moved to Toronto, Canada. After settling down and having been employed for four years Szakal decided to pursue her ambitions. She enrolled college and university programmes to upgrade her education, obtain training and supervision in mental health.

Szakal launched her private practice in Toronto in the year 2008 when she became a member of The Association of Registered Psychotherapists & Mental Health Professionals (O.A.C.C.P.P.), Dalton Associates, Psychological & Counselling Services in Ontario. Shortly after she joined GTA Psychological Services and extended her work from Greater Toronto Area throughout Halton and Waterloo Regions. With the development of distant and online services she has been working with many individuals from all walks of life, both in Canada and around the world.

Szakal's work grew into her passion. Her academic qualifications are augmented in certified training and extensive experience in the fields of education, psychotherapy, cognitive and behavioural therapy, mental imagery and mindfulness, all of which enforce and support her coaching credibility.

Szakal has been described as knowledgeable, empathetic, sensitive, and a good listener who is direct and forthright. She has a genuine and endearing personality that brings inspiration. Her expressed purpose has always been to help people experience the greatest possible fulfilment in their lives. She teaches how to restructure the mind to move forward, towards a better future.

APPENDIX

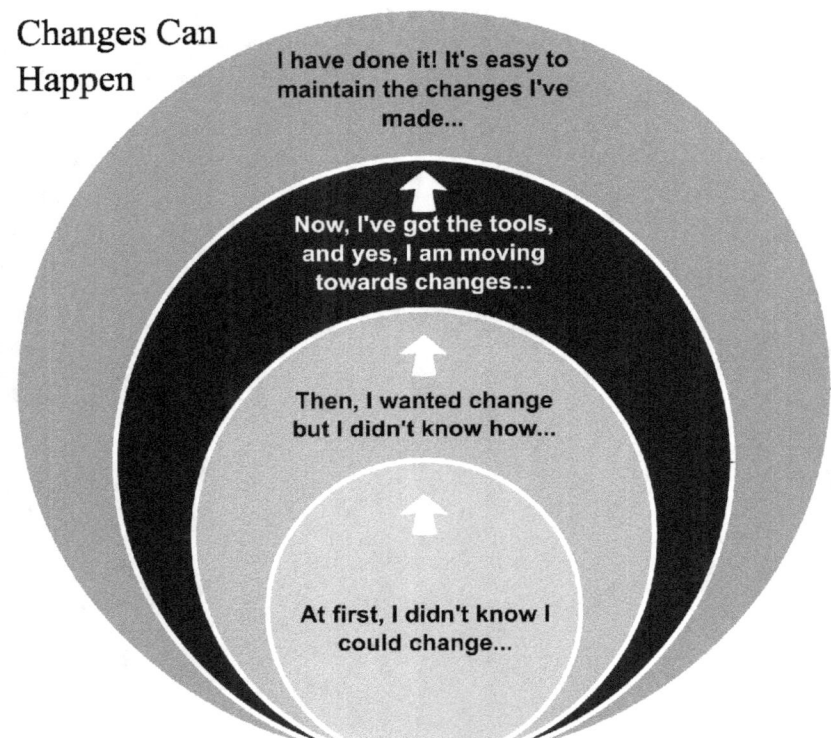

Daily Activities Log Week # __

	Day 1	Day 2	Day 3	Day 4	Day 5	Day 6	Day 7
Reading	✓ ✗	✓ ✗	✓ ✗	✓ ✗	✓ ✗	✓ ✗	✓ ✗
Journal	✓ ✗	✓ ✗	✓ ✗	✓ ✗	✓ ✗	✓ ✗	✓ ✗
Practice	✓ ✗	✓ ✗	✓ ✗	✓ ✗	✓ ✗	✓ ✗	✓ ✗
Total time							

Personal Statements:

Techniques / Tools:

Oops! Unplanned breach! What will I do to prevent it?

Weekly Summary

Positive Changes:

Unwanted Downfalls:

Oops! The negative mind! Strategy to overcome it in the future:

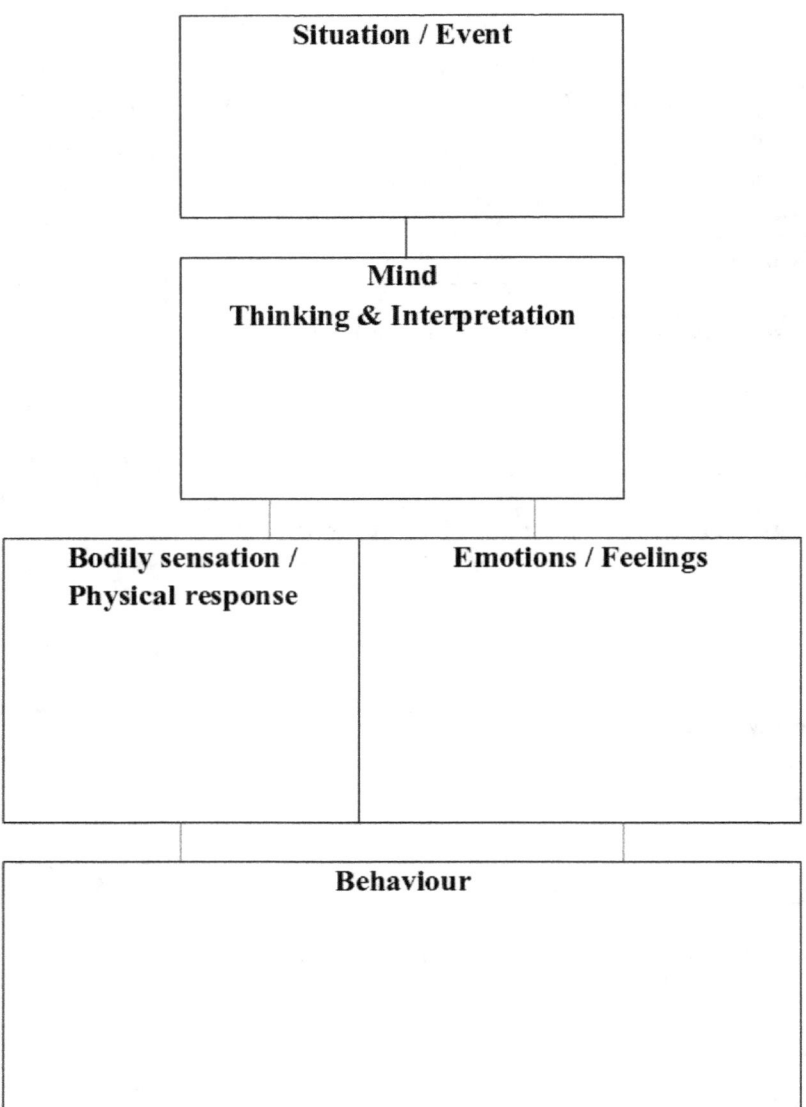

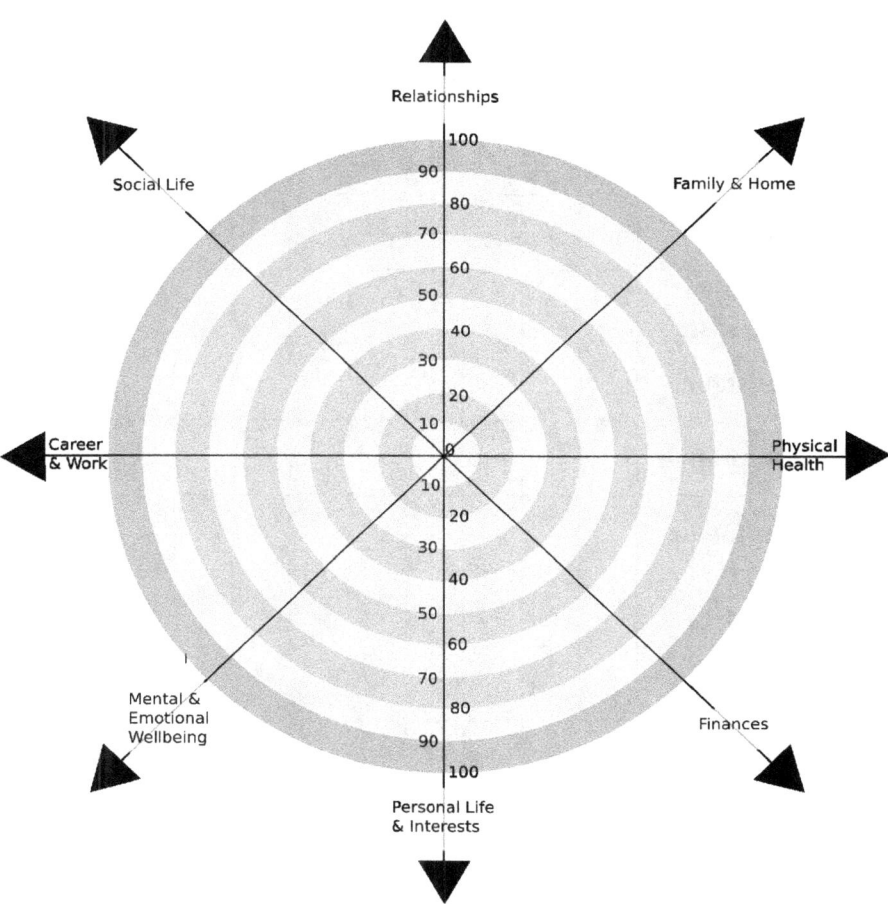

Area	weak					strong				
	1	2	3	4	5	6	7	8	9	10
Awareness										
Positive responses										
Resistance										
Acceptance										
Adaptability										
Copying										
Tolerance										
Ownership										
Flexibility										
Truthfulness										

Problematic patterns of thinking	Overall impact on emotions, feelings, motivation, problem resolving, behaviour and relationships
All or nothing	
Mental filter	
Jumping to conclusions	
Emotional reasoning and labelling	
Should, shouldn't, blame others and self-blame	

Situation – what happened, who was involved, where, why and when this happened
Thinking – self-talk before and during a situation, thoughts or mental images, expectations, judgements, beliefs
Feelings and emotions – feelings in the body, type of emotions, how strong emotions and feelings are
Interpretation of a situation and actions of people – understanding a situation and how reactions of an individual and other people was interpreted
Problematic thinking – using the list of dysfunctional thoughts identify the dysfunctional thoughts that affected interpretation and a situation as a whole
Finding the evidence
Evidence that supports thoughts - collecting truth and facts **Evidence that doesn't support thoughts or contradicts them** –collecting truth and facts
Alternative thinking – different viewpoints, wider perspective, open mind, non-judgemental thinking, what else could one think to change a situation?
New balanced interpretation and learning for future – based on evidence summarize different ways of thinking and interpreting, strategy for future

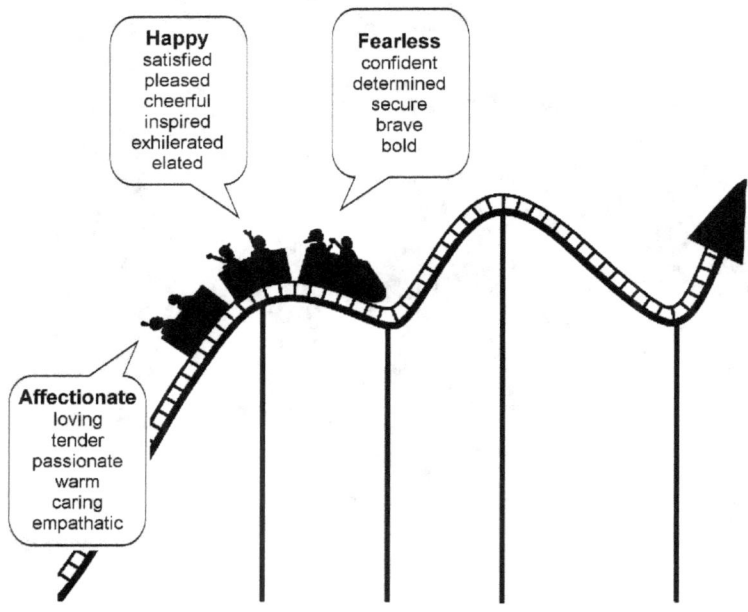

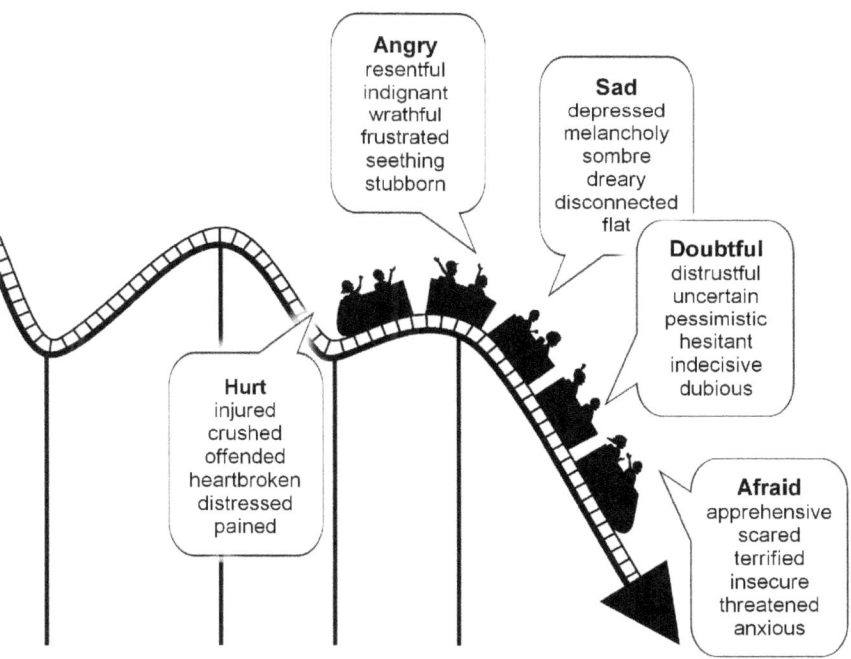

Belief:	
Costs	**Benefits**

Notes
Write about feelings, additional thoughts and problems caused by this belief

Problematic thoughts and beliefs	Emotions and feelings generated by them	Behaviour and actions triggered by them

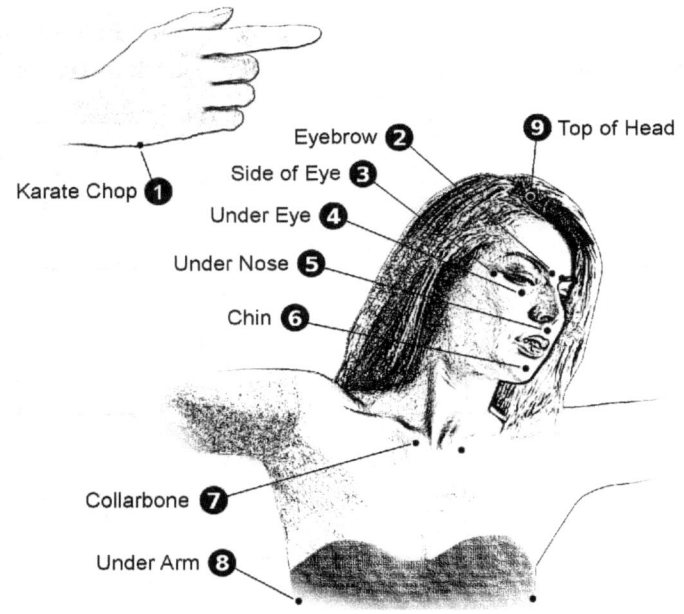

BIBLIOGRAPHY
Books

Beck, J. (2011). Cognitive therapy for challenging problems. The Guildford Press.
Brach, T. (2003). Radical acceptance: Embracing your life with the heart of a Buddha. Bantman Books.
Brewer, J. (2017). The craving mind.Yale University Press.
Burns, D. (1999). The feeling good: Handbook. Plume.
Burns, D. (2000). Ten days to great self-esteem. Random House.
Chambers, R., Ulbrich, M. (2016). Mindful relationships: Creating genuine connection with ourselves and others. Exisle Publishing.
Davenport, L. (2009). Healing and transformation through self-guided imagery. Celestial Arts.
Doidge, N: (2008). The brain that changes itself. Penguin Books Ltd.
Doidge, N. (2016). The brain's way of healing. Penguin Books Ltd.
Eifert, G. H., Forsyth, J. P. (2005). Acceptance and commitment therapy for anxiety disorders. New Harbinger Publications, Inc.
Frankl, V. (2004). The man's search for meaning. Penguin Random House. Ebury Publishing:
Hassed, C., McKenzie, S. (2012). Mindfulness for life. Exisle Publishing, Ltd.
Harris, R. (2008). The happiness trap: How to stop struggling and start living. Shambala Publications.
Hayes, S., Smith, S. (2005). Get out of your mind and into your life. New Harbinger Publications, Inc.
Hawks, J. W. (2010). Cell-level healing. Simon & Schuster, Inc.
Kabat-Zinn, J. (2005). Coming to our senses: Healing ourselves and the world through mindfulness. Piatkus Books, Ltd.
Kabat-Zinn, J. (2013). Full catastrophe living: Using the wisdom of your body and mind to face stress. Random House Publishing Group.
Naparstek, B. (2008). Staying well with guided imagery: How to harness the power of your imagination for health and healing. Warner Books.
Naparstek, B. (2009). Unlocking your sixth sense. Unlocking the power of your intuition. HarperCollins.
Neff, K. (2011). Self-compassion:Stop beating yourself up and leave insecurity behind. HarperCollins Publishers Inc.

O'Connor, J. (2005). Free yourself from fears: Overcoming anxiety and living without fear. Nicholas Brealey Publishing.

Rossman, M. (2000). Guided imagery for self-healing: An essential resource for anyone seeking wellness. New World Library.

Rossman, M. (2011). The worry solution. Penguin Random House. Ebury Publishing.

Thondap, T. (1998) The healing power of mind: Simple meditation exercises for health, well-being and enlightenment. Shambala Publications Boston & London.

Websites

www.feel-good.xyz/
www.normandoidge.com/
www.self-compassion.org/
www.smilingmind.com.au/
www.thestrongestyou.net/
www.umassmed.edu/cfm/

Other

Backgrounder: The relationship between mental health, mental illness and chronic physical conditions. Retrieved from: https://ontario.cmha.ca/documents/the-relationship-between-mental-health-mental-illness-and-chronic-physical-conditions/

Carver, J. Emotional memory management: Positive control over your memory. Retrieved from: http://counsellingresource.com/therapy/self-help/emotional-memory/5/

Hoffman, E. (October, 2005). Brain training against stress: Theory, methods and results from an outcome study. Mental fitness. Stress Report Version 4.2.

Rossman, M. How imagery works. Retrieved from: https://psychcentral.com/lib/how-imagery-works/

Mollick, L. What is behavioral activation? Retrieved from: http://nj-act.org/article16.html

IVANA STRASKA SAZAKAL

THE STRONGEST YOU

www.ingramcontent.com/pod-product-compliance
Lightning Source LLC
Chambersburg PA
CBHW070135080526
44586CB00015B/1701